Quiet Mind, Healthy Body

The ART of LOW-STRESS LIVING

Fu Faye
With appreciation
+ admiration —
Nancy

by

Nancy Tan, LCSW, E-RYT

FIG GARDEN PRESS

ISBN 978-0-615-18667-2

Printed in the United States

CONTENTS

To my mother,

who surrendered her own dreams

so mine might flourish.

ACKNOWLEDGMENTS

I would not have attempted this project except for my good fortune in having two friends, Lucy Phillips and Lesley Kellas Payne, who are not only professional editors but also women I trust to be truthful with me. Independently of each other over the years, both suggested I should write. Their encouragement went a long way in helping me develop confidence. Lesley also edited my first drafts and played a pivotal role in improving my writing skills.

Nor could I have written this book had it not been for the people who played crucial roles in my psychological integration. I thank my good friends Karla Baker, Brenda Tuttle, and Randy Janzen for their consistent love and support over the years. They listened to me when I was distressed, sat with me when I felt defeated, and rejoiced with me in my triumphs. Each served as a role model for me in her special way and helped shape who I am today.

Equally crucial to my integration as a person is Jim Doak, LCSW. I participated in Jim's Gestalt Therapy training group for over ten years. The group members learned to do psychotherapy by undergoing psychotherapy in the group. His patient interventions helped me uncover beliefs that trapped me in perpetual self-doubt, and his loving regard ignited my regard for myself.

I thank all the teachers with whom I have studied and the authors I have read. This book evolves from all I have learned from them. I thank my clients and my students. Without them I would only have intellectual and not experiential knowledge of the resourcefulness and resiliency of the human spirit.

I thank my family. My mother, whose life, due to political circumstances, was even more stressful and chaotic than mine, was a model of strength, integrity, and resiliency. Maturity clears my vision and I can now thank her, without ambivalence, for always wanting the best for me and from me. I thank my husband for his selfless support, not only of the writing of this book but in all I do. His kindness and generosity brings out my best. I thank my children for being the positive, loving individuals they are. I have not been a conventional mother, and their acceptance of me, as I am, is a precious gift.

It wasn't planned this way, but this book turned out to be a family project. My daughter Audrey, a certified Iyengar yoga instructor, is the model for the yoga poses. My husband, Rod, provided the illustrations. My sister Lilli Colton, a graphic artist and book designer, not only designed the cover and laid out the pages, but also supervised the printing. Thank you, Lilli, Rod, and Audrey, for enhancing the meaning of this book for me through this generous giving of yourselves. And many thanks as well to everyone who helped me narrow down the numerous choices for the book title.

Life is a continuous cycle of giving and receiving. Having received so much from others, it is my sincere hope that, through this book, I give back something of value. ❦

Nancy Tan
Fresno, California
January 2008

INTRODUCTION

*S*tress was not a word commonly used when I was growing up during the 1940s and 1950s. I remember life then as being slower and more gracious. People took breaks during the workday to rest, eat, or socialize. Working late was the exception rather than the rule. Families ate evening meals together regularly, and spent at least part of their weekends in recreation or relaxation.

Today stress is a household word. We use it to describe a certain harassed feeling we experience as we rush around. Taking a break during the workday seems out of vogue. People spend their lunchtime running errands, exercising, working at their desk, or meeting for business. The average family has lowered their aspiration to eat meals together to once or twice a week. The rest of the time, they grab food on the run or eat in shifts as they chauffeur themselves or their children from one activity to another.

Stress-induced illnesses are on the rise, although we don't always recognize or remember to acknowledge the stress factor in such conditions as anxiety states, depression, autoimmune dysfunctions, chronic pain, gastrointestinal disorders, heart disease, even cancer. While these conditions may seem out of our control, there are actually many things we can do to enhance our well-being and reduce our vulnerability to stress-related diseases. These include knowledge and awareness; an expanded repertoire of coping skills; a healthy lifestyle that promotes wellness; and a worldview and way of being that accords with our essential nature.

This book introduces exercises that can offer fairly immediate relief from stress. However, because symptom relief only provides a temporary solution, we also look at ways to improve the clarity of our perception so we can relate to the world around us more accurately, to manage our emotions so we can have peace of mind, and to understand and accept ourselves so we can create a lifestyle that is uniquely suitable for us. This long-range approach allows us to better deal with the stress that is an inherent part of life as well as avoid actions or inactions that might create more problems for us in the future.

Quiet Mind, Healthy Body draws from the ancient teachings of yoga, which include physical postures, breathing practices, meditation, and ethical guidelines. Yoga is a complete spiritual practice, but its genius lies in the fact that we can draw from it as little or as much as we are ready to take in. When I give talks on this subject, I frequently draw an analogy between yoga and the computer. We can use computers to do tasks such as word processing, accessing the Internet, or playing computer games, or we can use computers to accomplish incredible feats, such as guiding spacecraft to the moon. Likewise, we can incorporate yoga into a physical fitness regimen, we can make use of yoga's energetic properties to counteract anxiety, stress, or depression, or we can embrace its teachings in its entirety as a path to self-realization.

This book also draws from the teachings of Ayurveda, which is yoga's sister science in that both are rooted in ancient Vedic teachings from India. It is possibly the world's first holistic, energy-based system for self-healing. It offers guidelines for daily living to keep us in optimal health, and its teachings are particularly pertinent for chronic conditions since it addresses the entire person, not just their symptoms.

I believe it is not by accident that yoga has gained such popularity within the last few years, and that Ayurveda and other alternative medicines are also rapidly gaining recognition. Organisms have an inherent ability to know what they need, and I believe that we are drawn to these ancient healing arts during these increasingly stressful times because we intuitively recognize them as paths that can lead us back to wholeness.

In drawing from both yoga and Ayurveda, I have purposely refrained from using Sanskrit terms or going too deeply into theoretical under-pinnings because I want this book to serve as a practical guide that is simple to read, understand, and implement. Too much information can be stressful in itself. I have included a list of suggested resources at the end of the book for those who would like to study these teach-ings in more depth. To avoid information overload, and also because I believe our culture needs to bring an overdeveloped intellect and an underdeveloped intuitive way of functioning into better balance, I have not placed a heavy emphasis on research data. My suggestions can all be verified through the reader's own experience, a far better way to proceed, since this turning inward simultaneously encourages the development of awareness, a key ingredient in reducing stress.

Another source from which this book draws heavily is my experience as a psychotherapist for almost thirty years, the last fifteen of which have been spent specializing in working with people suffering from stress-related conditions. I have drawn on what I have learned about stress physiology and psychological principles of human develop-ment, my training in humanistic and transpersonal psychotherapies, and my studies in Buddhist philosophy, energy healing, and other modalities of alternative healing arts. I feel truly blessed that my varied interests and fields of study, which at times seemed divergent, can now coalesce and become part of a cohesive whole. ❧

While we cannot control life,

we can alter how we relate to its vicissitudes.

CHAPTER 1

WHAT STRESS IS AND HOW IT WORKS

Stress has become a common household word—even children use it to describe unpleasant experiences. Perhaps such common usage has diluted the meaning of the word, dangerously minimizing the actual physical and psychological impact of chronic stress, the progression of which is insidious and difficult to recognize. It is important, therefore, to define this one-syllable word and develop a better understanding of its numerous implications for daily living. Even more importantly, we must become more skilled in our ability to recognize stress as it occurs. Only through this combination of awareness and understanding can we take an active role in keeping ourselves well. Sadly, whether we are aware of it or not, most of us experience this modern-day malady in one form or another far more often than we might think.

WHAT IS STRESS?

When we think of stress, our tendency is to see it as something outside of ourselves happening to us, to see ourselves as passive recipients. We associate stress with events such as death, divorce, relocation, loss of income, an argument, or an embarrassing situation. Yet, even though some events are widely acknowledged as being stressful, our individual responses to a given situation can vary considerably. An event or experience that is highly stressful for one person, for example, may not be as stressful to another; certain situations, such as social gatherings, public speaking, or performing in public, might be stressful for some people but enjoyed by others.

Our personal response to a specific stressful situation also tends to vary from one occasion to the next. For example, we are more likely to react negatively to work-related stress when we are going through difficult times in our personal lives than when our lives are proceeding smoothly. Or, we might become more easily irritated with our loved ones when our work is extra demanding. Handling new or difficult situations can feel more stressful if there are many other demands competing for our time and energy. Likewise, something we take in stride once or twice may begin to feel more and more difficult to cope with when it continues or recurs.

Given these variables, it would be more accurate to think of stress as a dynamic interaction between a particular situation and the individual's present state of resiliency, habitual patterns of perception, and repertoire of coping skills. In other words, the degree to which we feel stressed depends on how much stress we are already under, how we perceive the stress-inducing situation, and whether we have the necessary skills to deal with the stress. This definition of stress acknowledges that we have some say in the degree of stress we experience. This acknowledgment is crucial in managing stress because it puts us back in the driver's seat. While we cannot control what life brings us, we can set realistic limits on the amount of stress we incur at any given time, learn to clear and expand our perception, and expand our repertoire of coping skills. It is important to understand that when it comes to our quality of life, we play a much larger role than we might think, and this knowledge alone has some stress-relieving value.

THE STRESS RESPONSE
The stress response is governed by our autonomic nervous system, which controls the body's involuntary processes, such as respiration, blood pressure, heart rate, and body temperature. There are

two parts to the autonomic nervous system: the sympathetic nervous system regulates the stress response, and the parasympathetic nervous system controls the relaxation response. In this chapter we discuss the effects of the stress response on our physiology and develop an understanding of the relationship between these physiological changes and chronic illnesses. Subsequent chapters draw from the traditions of Ayurveda and yoga as well as contemporary psychology to address how to evoke the relaxation response of the parasympathetic system and restore equilibrium.

Our sympathetic nervous system prepares us for emergencies so we can respond rapidly in a manner that is appropriate to the situation. When we sense danger, the stress response automatically puts us into a *fight or flight* mode. Adrenaline is discharged into the bloodstream, affecting every organ in the body as we prepare to survive the perceived threat; the heart pumps faster; the breath moves primarily into the chest; blood sugar rises to provide extra fuel; and blood vessels constrict to direct blood flow into the extremities and the brain. This state of emergency can enable us to accomplish amazing things, such as finding the inordinate strength to lift a heavy vehicle off of an accident victim, or surviving incredible dangers through heightened vigilance and endurance. As we will see, however, this same mechanism for self-preservation can, under certain circumstances, compromise our health.

AN EXAMPLE OF THE STRESS RESPONSE

Many years ago I verbally expelled a masked, knife-wielding intruder from my home. I was incredibly calm during the experience, as though I were a bystander watching myself act and speak. After the acute danger had passed, however, my body shook uncontrollably for over an hour. At the time the shaking frightened me even more than the intruder had. I felt as though I had lost control of my body. Now I understand that the reaction was my body's response to the residual stress hormones that had been released to help me deal with the terrifying situation. Shaking and trembling are common physical reactions to acute stress. We acknowledge this phenomenon when we say, "I was so scared (or angry or upset) that I was shaking."

STRESS IN CONTEMPORARY TIMES

The fight or flight response has been with us since prehistoric times. The same response kicked into gear for our ancestors when they battled marauders or fled from saber-toothed tigers. Their sympathetic nervous systems released adrenaline into the bloodstream, and the physiological changes helped them survive. Because the threats they faced tended to be ones that literally endangered their lives, increased physical exertion was required of them, whether fleeing or fighting. This physical activity utilized the stress hormones dispensed into their system.

Our fight or flight response today tends to be triggered far less frequently by actual physical danger than by a multitude of perceived psychological threats, such as a traffic jam delaying us when we have an important business meeting, the stock market taking a downturn, fierce competition for a promotion, a demanding sales quota, the risk of displeasing a superior at work, or conflict with a loved one. While these stressors might pale next to marauders and saber-toothed tigers, they nevertheless set off our alarm system and release stress hormones into our bloodstream.

Whatever might be lacking in the magnitude of these psychological threats is usually more than amply compensated for by their frequency. In fact, these triggering events in our lives today are so plentiful that they can be almost continuous, and they generally leave us with neither adequate ways to utilize the excess stress hormones nor sufficient time between threats to restore equilibrium. In time this situation compromises our physical and emotional well-being.

CHRONIC STRESS

Our physiology is designed to easily withstand occasional stress. After a crisis, a built-in mechanism restores us to our original state, called homeostasis. An accumulation of stress over time, especially without sufficient time for recovery, compromises the homeostatic mechanism, dulls our senses, and impairs our ability to respond appropriately. If a live frog is thrown into a pot of boiling water the frog will immediately jump out and save itself. However, if the same frog is placed in a pot of cold water that is heated slowly, the frog will adjust to the slowly rising water temperature and complacently allow itself to be boiled to death. In this situation, the same mechanisms for maintaining homeostasis, meant to enable the frog to adapt to a wide range of temperatures and thereby increase its chances for survival, actually contribute to its destruction.

The homeostatic mechanism in human beings creates a similar self-destructive effect in response to the slowly rising heat of chronic stress. We become less and less in tune with what is good for us as our senses become dulled. Symptoms of stress such as chronic muscular tension, headaches, insomnia, fatigue, digestive-tract disturbances, hypertension, anxiety, and depression can actually begin to feel normal. The barrage of advertisements for remedies for these stress-induced symptoms is a strong indication of the prevalence of chronic stress in our society today; far too many people are accommodating these symptoms as a normal part of their daily lives.

Even worse, there is a widespread tendency to mistake symptom relief for true remedy, and the advertising industry compounds this misunderstanding by presenting its clients' products as effective solutions. Instead of reading symptoms as our body's way of letting us know that something is wrong and out of balance, we reach for a quick fix to rid ourselves of the symptoms. Taking a pill to reduce acidity in the stomach or getting a shot to alleviate muscular pain does not address the underlying problems that might be causing these symptoms, such as food toxins or poor posture. It is critical that we understand this vital distinction and not compromise our expectations as to what constitutes wellness.

As we will see, there are many strategies we can use to keep ourselves well. However, these efforts require our attention and time, which people leading fast-paced lives are loath to expend on themselves. This tendency to favor quick solutions is short-sighted and does not serve us well. When we ignore warning signs from our body, we forego the opportunity to take timely and appropriate action and seriously risk compromising our health and well-being.

CHRONIC STRESS AND CHRONIC ILLNESSES

We experience stress anytime the demands on us require that we stretch beyond our usual comfort zone. When the required effort is within a manageable range and we receive the support we need, we can respond to the situation appropriately and feel successful. The experience becomes growth enhancing because it expands our repertoire of skills and helps us gain confidence in our ability to meet life's challenges. If the demands are excessive, however, or if we do not have adequate support, we are likely to feel over-whelmed and inadequate and lose confidence in our abilities. When excessive demands continue over an extended period of time, stress becomes chronic and the likelihood of our succumbing to stress-induced symptoms increases dramatically.

Knowing how the stress response affects our physiology helps us understand why certain chronic conditions are considered stress-related. The bodily processes of the stress response and the chemicals released, intended to serve a purpose, become harmful to us under chronic stress because they have neither the time nor the natural avenues to be neutralized. The constant presence of stress hormones in the bloodstream, for example, affects the white blood cells, eventually suppressing immune function and increasing our vulnerability to infections and autoimmune diseases. Frequently elevated blood pressure and blood sugar increase our risk for hypertension and diabetes. The thickening of platelets in our blood for quick coagulation, should we be wounded, eventually leads to blockages in our arteries, setting the stage for heart attacks and strokes. When blood flow is shunted away from the center of the body, digestion suffers. Since digestion is the foundation of good health, chronic digestive problems can't help but lead to a multitude of ills.

Besides its direct impact on physiology, a fast-paced, stressful lifestyle also contributes indirectly to poor health. Harried people are less likely to take the time to shop for fresh ingredients and cook for themselves. Indeed, we have come to rely more and more on fast food, restaurant meals, and highly processed prepackaged foods, all of which contain more fat, sodium, and chemicals than is good for our physical health. I noticed during a group hike not long ago that I was the only one of eight people who brought what I laughingly called "real food" for lunch, a sandwich in this case. Everyone else pulled out energy bars, which are highly processed and made with doubtful ingredients but successfully marketed as "healthy."

Chronic stress also compromises our muscular-skeletal systems. In the field of physics, stress is defined as "an applied force or system of forces that tends to strain or deform a body." Under prolonged stress, our bodies are subjected to forces that inevitably leave a straining or deforming effect. People who have lived under chronic stress for a long period, for example, tend to carry themselves with raised shoulders hunched over a collapsed chest. This posture creates anatomical stress in a variety of ways. The rounding of the shoulders and upper back makes it necessary, in order to see, to jut our head forward out of alignment with the spinal column. The neck and shoulder muscles must work overtime to keep the head upright, resulting in chronic neck and shoulder tension. The lungs are compressed, and we no longer breathe to our full capacity, compromising our sense of vitality. This posture also causes the lower back to round, resulting in lower-back pain and potential injury to the spinal discs.

RECOGNIZING STRESS

Stress manifests itself differently in each of us. Some of us might sleep excessively when under stress; others might suffer from insomnia. Some of us might lose our appetite, others might overeat. There may also be variations in our individual responses to stress. For example, we might lose our appetite under extreme stress but overeat when the stress we experience is less severe. Becoming irritable or agitated, withdrawn or depressed, even anxious to the point of having panic attacks and phobias are all possible responses to stress.

We experience stress far more frequently than we might realize. Because our lives feel so familiar to us, we tend to take our experiences for granted and not examine them objectively in terms of the true impact they have on us. This makes it easy for stress to accumulate and become chronic. Since we can only heal what we are aware of, it is important to periodically take time to stop, tune in, and notice. Besides the symptoms mentioned above, we might also notice whether we are holding our breath, clenching our jaws, or tensing our shoulders. We can take stock of whether we have been feeling more irritated about things we normally take in stride, whether we feel more fatigued, and whether it has been more difficult to get things done. On a more general level, we might ask ourselves whether we feel alive and vital, and whether our lives are satisfying and meaningful.

It is helpful to familiarize ourselves with common stress-inducing situations so we can better recognize them when they occur. Stress accumulates when our life moves at an unnaturally fast tempo. When we chronically rush, overwork, multitask, and do not get sufficient sleep and rest, stress becomes an ongoing, low-grade source of aggravation from which we have no respite. More alarmingly, we come to consider this fast-paced life normal, and our expectations of ourselves become unrealistic. When we feel rightfully overwhelmed, we are more likely to think there is something wrong with us than with the situation, and to compound our problems with self-recrimination. I refer to this compounding of problems as "self-induced stress" because it can be avoided.

I have noticed in my psychotherapy practice that one of the functions I have come to perform more and more frequently over the last few decades is that of serving as a surrogate stress thermometer for people whose own gauges no longer measure their stress level accurately. Women in particular carry inordinate loads, frequently pulling double duty at work and at home. Many parents work more hours than ever before, while being involved in more extracurricular activities with their children than ever before. In such a societal climate, it is critical that we turn inward and monitor our reserves so we can set realistic limits on excessive demands of our time and energy.

Certain professions that present actual physical danger, such as law enforcement, firefighting, and the military, naturally generate stress. Professions that function within an adversarial system, such as law, also generate high stress since we are harmonious beings by nature and conflict goes against our grain. Professions that routinely require excessively high outputs of energy and time, such as management and law, or entail maintaining hours that are not in accord with nature, such as shift work, tax our resources. Situations according a high degree of responsibility but not the necessary authority, as can happen in middle management and in stepparenting, create more stress than situations in which the lines of responsibility and authority are clearly drawn. Some life situations, such as single parenting or caring for an aging or chronically ill family member, especially without the support of an extended family or larger community, are highly stressful. Because we are social beings by nature, feeling isolated and lacking connections to like-minded people can also create stress.

STRESS TOLERANCE

Because chronic stress impairs our resiliency to stress, those of us who grew up in chronically stressful situations frequently have a decreased stress tolerance. This means we might more likely perceive situations to be stressful or succumb more easily to stress. Family circumstances that are chronically stressful include those where there is a high degree of conflict; where expectations are overly high; where there is inadequate supervision and support; where love is experienced as conditional; where life is chaotic; where boundaries are unclear; where discipline is overly harsh or arbitrary; where roles are reversed and children assume the emotional care of their parents; where a family member drinks excessively, routinely uses drugs, or suffers from a chronic illness; or where there is physical, psychological, or sexual abuse. These situations, when unmitigated by support from a responsible and caring adult, whether a relative, neighbor, or teacher, leave us with inadequate skills to calm ourselves or ask for help when we need it.

To complicate matters, children tend to take their experiences for granted and do not fully comprehend the extent to which they are being affected. They tend to see their increased vulnerability to stress as proof of their inherent inadequacy. This perception hinders their ability to be compassionate with themselves or see themselves as capable of taking steps to strengthen their stress tolerance.

These fears, left unaddressed, can carry over into adulthood. Jenny, for example, worried constantly, felt timid in new situations, and feared change. She was passive in her relationships and frequently felt overwhelmed by situations that others took in stride. Jenny felt there was something wrong with her, which added to her insecurities. Jenny's mother suffered from severe anxiety, and Jenny's childhood was filled with warnings about imagined dangers. Incongruously, she was also frequently left alone. She recalled feeling frightened, lost, and lonely, without an adult to offer support and comfort. These are feelings and memories Jenny had filed away and forgotten until she began therapy, but which continued to affect her in major ways.

STRESS-EXACERBATING COPING PATTERNS
Responses that are effective for dealing with a particular stressful situation are not always functional or appropriate in other circumstances.

Always being submissive, for example, could be lifesaving when growing up with an abusive parent but not functional in later relationships with peers or one's spouse. When a stressful situation is chronic, a particular way of coping can develop into a pattern of behavior that, no longer in our awareness, kicks into gear automatically. Not being able to set limits or speak up on our own behalf, flaring up in anger when we feel thwarted, and needing to be perfect in all we do are but a few examples of these patterns. Gestalt Therapy refers to them as "creative adaptations." They were effective and functional coping mechanisms under the original circumstances but they now keep us trapped in patterns that cause more problems than they solve, adding avoidable stress to our lives.

SELF-ACCEPTANCE

Since the first step in any transformation is to become aware of what is, the following awareness exercise helps us identify some of the common patterns that no longer serve us well. When we begin to look more deeply into our patterns, however, it is important to do so with a loving and nonjudgmental attitude toward ourselves, to see these patterns as the result of our resourcefulness rather than our inadequacies. Self-acceptance is a theme that is emphasized throughout this book, for it is the essential attitude for reducing stress. Not accepting ourselves is actually a stress-inducing behavior pattern that is no longer functional.

Contrary to misconception, accepting ourselves does not mean we like everything about ourselves. What it does mean is that we come to terms with all aspects of ourselves. We do not berate ourselves for the things we do not like, disown them by pretending they do not exist, or displace responsibility for them by blaming others for how we are. We acknowledge all that we learn about ourselves and decide what we can live with and what we would like to work on. Paradoxically, self-acceptance is the precursor to any constructive change, since we cannot change anything of which we refuse to take ownership.

AWARENESS EXERCISE

Check the patterns below that apply to you. Take the time to recall a few stressful situations you have experienced as a result of each of the patterns you checked. Remember how you felt so you can truly understand their ramifications. Begin to catch yourself in these patterns, and decide consciously in each situation, or in retrospect, whether a different response might serve you better. Note that response and file it away as a possibility for the future. The more aware you become and the more alternative responses you collect, the more you will be able to make conscious choices. For the patterns marked with an asterisk, I offer practical suggestions to facilitate your changing these patterns immediately, should you so desire.

Some of the ways I try to cope that may actually exacerbate my stress include:

- ☐ Giving more consideration to how other people feel or want than to my own preferences and desires
- ☐ Not setting limits or saying "no" for fear of not being liked *
- ☐ Refusing to ask for help for fear of being turned down or thought badly of
- ☐ Avoiding being a "problem," to the extent of turning down the help I need
- ☐ Rising to the occasion without considering my own needs **
- ☐ Procrastinating and avoiding certain situations even though the avoidance may cause me a bigger problem later
- ☐ Cramming in as much as possible whenever I have a free moment

☐ Thinking of all the possible negative outcomes when faced with choices, and feeling increasingly anxious, discouraged, or immobilized

☐ Feeling bad about myself when I experience certain feelings, such as anger, hurt, or humiliation

☐ Expecting myself to be perfect

SUGGESTIONS

* When you begin to set limits and say no to requests, keep your responses short and simple. The mantra here could be, "That won't work for me." Resist the impulse to give explanations. While your intention in explaining is to soften the imagined impact on the other person, lengthy explanations actually tend to have the opposite effect. Put yourself in the other's place and notice whether you want a barrage of reasons for saying no, or whether a simple but kind refusal would feel better to you.

Certain circumstances might warrant a short and simple explanation. In those situations, something truthful and personal, such as, "Sundays are my day of rest," "My schedule has been so full that I can't take on one more thing," or "I am not good with children and I find babysitting too stressful" will serve you far better than using external circumstances, because external circumstances can be reasoned away, while your preferences and desires cannot. Remember that the people you would like to have in your life are those who are respectful of your limits.

Sometimes it is difficult for us to refuse a request because we do not allow ourselves to ask for help until we are desperate. Setting limits for others helps us understand that limit-setting is about taking care of ourselves, not about the other person having overstepped their bounds by asking. With this understanding we can more easily accept a refusal from others without taking it as a personal affront, and we are also apt to ask for the assistance we need from others more frequently.

** A useful phrase for people with the tendency to rise to the occasion is, "Let me think about it." This response allows us the time we need for conscious decisionmaking. Tap into your internal responses, such as excitement, willingness, reluctance, or dread, and allow them a proper place in your consideration as to the course of action that will best serve you. Sometimes we have to do what we would rather not do, but doing so as a conscious decision, with a clear understanding of the reasons we made our choice, is a different experience from simply succumbing to all requests by repeating an unconscious pattern. Also remember that you always have the right to change your mind when you find that you have overextended yourself, as long as you extricate yourself responsibly.

SUMMARY

Stress is a simple process of physiology that becomes complex and multifaceted when it is chronic. A physiological response that has served us well since time immemorial has evolved into a major health threat in our fast-paced society. Chronic stress troubles most of us, but it is far more difficult to recognize and own than it would appear at first glance. Understanding that our personal response to a stressful situation can change how much it affects us and identifying personal coping patterns that actually increase our stress load puts us back into the driver's seat. While we cannot control what life brings us, we can change ourselves in these respects, thereby making our lives significantly easier. ♣

We can do without food and water for many days,

but we will not survive even a few minutes without breath.

CHAPTER 2

BREATHE YOUR STRESS AWAY

*N*ow that we understand the dynamics of stress and their impact on us, we can turn our attention to remedies. The good news is that immediate stress relief is readily available. Breath, something we usually take for granted and therefore ignore, gives us direct access to our nervous system. When we join our awareness to our breath, we trigger our relaxation response and quickly calm ourselves down. There is a saying that is worth remembering: "Where our consciousness travels, breath follows, and healing begins." This chapter offers a simple explanation of how our breath works and introduces breathing exercises that can offer instant relief. Try them and find out for yourself how your breath, which is always accessible to you, can be your best stress reliever.

BREATH

The breath is the marker of our life span. Our life begins with our first inhalation at the time of our birth, and ends with our last exhalation at the time of our death. We can do without food and water for many days, but we will not survive even a few minutes without breath. When we consider this, the importance of our breath takes on awesome proportions. Yet breathing is something most of us take for granted. We notice our breath infrequently. The relationship between our sense of vitality and our capacity to breathe fully has largely become lost in our society, as has the knowledge that we can manage our moods by modulating our breath.

THE IMPACT OF STRESS ON BREATHING

When we are relaxed, our breath is naturally slow, deep, and rhythmic. This is the natural breathing pattern that is our birthright. If we were to watch a baby asleep on his back, we would see that his belly noticeably expands when he breathes in, and retracts and falls as he breathes out, smoothly and rhythmically. Chronic stress has not yet set in to disrupt his breathing pattern.

Our emotions affect the way we breathe. When we are frightened, challenged, startled, or tense, we either hold our breath or breathe shallowly. In shallow breathing, the breath travels only a short distance, gathering primarily in our upper chest cavity rather than moving further down into the diaphragm. The upper chest rises and falls, but the ribs and abdomen remain relatively still. References to the relationship between emotions and breath are common in the English language. We say we "held our breath" while waiting in suspense, we were left "breathless" by some event, or we were so fearful we were "barely breathing."

Our posture also affects our breath, and stress affects our posture. When we feel weighed down by stress, we have a tendency to slump forward. When we slump, whether standing or sitting, our shoulders begin to roll forward, and our upper and middle back begins to round. In such a rounded position, we are collapsing against the lungs and reducing our ability to breathe. When our posture is chronically slumped, in time it becomes difficult to keep our spine erect. The muscles that hold us upright become weakened and imbalanced in the direction of the slump. The fascia, a thin layer of fibrous tissue that envelops the body beneath the surface of the skin, becomes molded to the slump and acts like a suit of armor.

For people who have been subjected to prolonged stress, shallow breathing becomes a habitual pattern. This manner of breathing utilizes only a small portion of our lung capacity and does not provide us with the optimal amount of oxygen. As a result, we might experience less vitality and more fatigue or depression. We might also feel short of breath and mildly anxious. In fact, people who suffer from chronic anxiety and panic attacks are frequently shallow breathers, and their shallow breathing pattern reinforces their feelings of anxiety and panic.

CONSCIOUS BREATHING

Breathing is a bodily function that is both automatic and subject to our conscious influence. When we pay attention to our breathing, we find we can influence our breath and make amazing things happen. For example, we can breathe faster or slower, deeper or shallower, softer or harder—all of which are patterns that have different effects on our physiology.

Breathing with awareness is a process that differs substantively from breathing automatically, without awareness. Conscious breathing links our body and mind and allows healing to take place on multiple levels. It gives us direct access to our nervous system, and it can change the quality of our consciousness. Slow, deep, rhythmic, and conscious breathing soothes our nervous system and initiates the relaxation response by shutting down the sympathetic nervous system and putting the parasympathetic nervous system back in charge.

The first and most important task in counteracting stress, therefore, is to free our breath from chronic restrictions and restore a normal breathing pattern. This can be accomplished by increasing breath awareness. The simple task of focusing our awareness on our breath will help us re-establish our normal breathing pattern and allow healing to begin.

PARAMETERS FOR PRACTICE

The two exercises presented in this chapter are for increasing breath awareness. I recommend initially setting aside fifteen to twenty minutes twice a day to practice them. It is necessary to specifically schedule the time for the exercises. This is an important appointment you make with yourself to improve the quality of your life. Intentions to "fit it in" when your schedule is already over-flowing seldom come to fruition. Bedtime can be an excellent time for one of the practice sessions, since these exercises can help alleviate insomnia. They are far more constructive and less frustrating than just lying there and worrying about not sleeping.

This commitment of time may seem impossible when your life already feels too full, but conscious breathing becomes a habit very quickly and can then be incorporated into your day without extra time commitments. For the purpose of calming the nervous system, continue these exercises until normal breathing is the rule rather than the exception, until you notice that conscious breathing has become a familiar tool for dealing with stress during your day. Be forewarned, however, that you may find having quiet time to yourself so pleasurable that you will want to keep this time open for other practices that enhance growth and reduce stress.

It is important that you allow sufficient time to transition in and out of this time you have set aside for yourself. Rushing through these exercises and glancing at your watch the whole time only creates more stress. A resolution to engage in this one activity in a more leisurely manner will be a significant step toward changing stress-inducing habits in favor of better self-care. I periodically have to remind my students that rushing into a yoga class five minutes late and rushing off again before the ending relaxation is contrary to the spirit of yoga practice and self-care.

In the same vein as allowing sufficient transition time, it is important to eliminate interruptions during the time you have set aside. Family matters and telephone calls can wait. This is a courtesy you would accord to a meeting with someone you respect, and this time with yourself deserves the same consideration. Setting these boundaries for the time you take to care for yourself is an essential part of creating a less stressful lifestyle.

Once you have made these commitments to yourself, find a quiet, relaxing place to do these exercises. Our environment affects us more than we sometimes realize. A carpeted floor is preferable since it provides some cushioning and warmth. If you are practicing on a hard surface, be sure to lay down several layers of blankets. Soothing music can enhance your experience, and the tracks on a CD can also serve as a timer so you can relax completely and immerse yourself in the experience.

EXERCISE 1—Breathing from the Center

1. Lie face down on the floor with a firm pillow or folded blanket under your abdomen horizontally so you can rest comfortably on your stomach without strain to your neck. Make sure the pillow is not under your diaphragm, since that would hinder your breathing. People with lower-back issues often find it helpful to have another pillow under their shins.

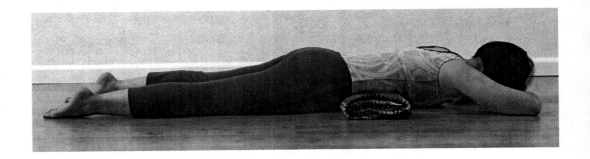

2. Bend your elbows and place your hands on top of each other so they can serve as a cushion for your head. You can either rest your forehead on your hands or turn your head to one side and rest your cheek on your hands, whichever is more comfortable for you.

3. It is important to take a moment and pay attention to yourself and make certain that you do not feel any strain in your neck. Making the pillow higher or placing a rolled towel under your ankles can sometimes create greater ease. You must feel completely comfortable for this exercise to be beneficial, since discomfort inhibits the breath.

4. Close your eyes and tune in to your breathing. Become aware of the rising and falling of your abdomen as you breathe. You might notice your abdomen pressing into the pillow more as you inhale, and less when you exhale. Imagine that you are the baby mentioned earlier, your abdomen expanding and receding as you breathe in and out. Allow yourself to rest deeply in this awareness for at least five minutes.

5. Now shift your awareness to the back of your body. Notice that the back of your body also rises and falls as you breathe. You might find that the breath spreads outward from around the mid-back,

possibly in several patterns. Notice the responding subtle movements along your spine. Rest deeply into this awareness for at least five minutes. You are likely to find your attention wandering during this time. This is quite common. When it happens, simply bring your attention back to your breath and pick up where you left off.

EXERCISE 2—The Three-Part Breath

This exercise is longer, with more components. You might initially want to enlist the help of a friend with a calming voice and manner to read the instructions to you, or set up a buddy system and do this for each other. Another possibility is to read the instructions into a tape recorder for yourself, speaking slowly and calmly.

1. Lie comfortably on your back on the floor. If you experience strain in your lower back, use a cushion or rolled-up blankets under your knees for support. If your chin tilts up toward the ceiling, place a folded blanket or towel under your head so that your neck extends naturally, with its normal curve intact.

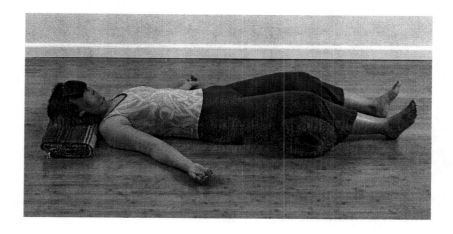

2. Feel your body weight on the floor and make any necessary adjustments so that you are lying symmetrically along your spine. It is important that you take the time to experience your body and make the necessary adjustments so that you are completely comfortable. Discomfort in the body inhibits the breath.

3. Now close your eyes and begin to pay attention to your breathing. Do not try to change anything right now, since you are just gathering information. Notice where in your body you tend to primarily breathe, whether it is the abdomen, ribs, or chest. Also notice the quality of your breath, whether it is shallow or deep, smooth or restricted in places. Notice whether you can inhale and exhale with similar ease. If not, which is more difficult? If, as you are observing, your breath changes its pattern, just allow that to take place.

4. Now place one hand and your awareness on your abdomen. Without trying to force anything, see if you can gently guide your breath there. Imagine that your inhalations are riding an elevator down toward the abdomen. Feel the abdomen rise and fall under your hand, and notice what it feels like to breathe primarily from the abdomen. Is it familiar? Breathe this way for a few rounds, until breathing into the abdomen begins to feel familiar.

5. Move both hands up to your ribs. Place your hands on the sides of your torso so that the fingers as well as the thumbs are facing each other and the heels of your hands are resting lightly on your rib cage. Gently guide your breath there. Notice how your fingers separate from each other as your ribs expand when you breathe in and come back together again when you breathe out. Notice what it is like to breathe primarily from the ribs, and continue breathing this way for a few rounds, until this pattern of breathing begins to feel familiar.

6. Now place one hand on your chest and gently guide your breath there. Allow the breath to spread across your upper chest, spreading your collarbones away from each other. Notice what is feels like to breathe primarily from the chest and whether this is familiar to you. Breathe here for a few rounds.

7. Finally, place one hand on your abdomen and one hand on your chest. As you inhale, guide your breath first to the abdomen and allow it to fill, then spilling naturally into the diaphragm, and finally to the chest. When you exhale, allow the chest to empty first, then the diaphragm, and then the belly. At the end of the exhalation, notice how the abdomen might contract a little, expelling the last bit of air out.

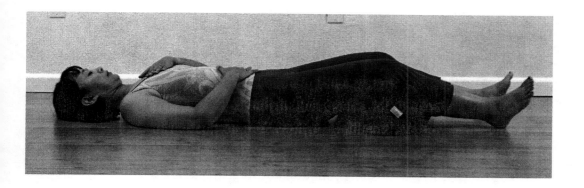

8. Experience this wave-like action of your breath as you continue to breathe in this pattern for a few more rounds. Always feel free to return to your normal breathing for a few breaths whenever you feel the need, so that you feel no strain. Should your mind wander, simply bring it back to the task at hand.

9. Now rest quietly in your normal breathing, and observe any effects this exercise may have had.

BREATH BREAKS

For our efforts to be truly helpful to us, it is important that we integrate what we learn into our everyday life. Breathing exercises teach us how to breathe and quiet an overwrought nervous system. Stopping and paying attention to your breathing periodically throughout the day makes conscious breathing a tool that you can draw on during times of need. These little breathing breaks take only seconds and are excellent ways to keep your stress level down and your emotions steady.

During these breaks, consciously send your breath to the belly and help your breath become slow, deep, and rhythmic. This takes no extra time, since you are breathing anyhow. You are just paying attention. To help you remember, you can link these breaks to regular activities, such as brushing your teeth, getting in and out of your car, eating, answering the phone, or stopping at a traffic light. On the computer, you can even program reminders for yourself to take mini breathing breaks throughout the day. You will be surprised how effective conscious breathing can be in helping you stay calm and balanced. In time you will automatically draw on conscious breathing when you are facing stressful events.

SUMMARY

Breath awareness is something all of us can easily practice, anytime, anywhere, without any special equipment. By reaching our nervous system directly, conscious breathing quickly and effectively changes our physiology. Not only will you feel less stressed, but over time, you might also be pleasantly surprised to find yourself less reactive and better able to respond to situations proactively. However, no matter how effective these exercises can be for relieving stress, they work only when done faithfully. Believe that nothing can be more important, more imminent than your physical and psychological well-being. Make a commitment to your wellness by making and keeping these important appointments with your breath. 🍂

Time for rest and renewal should be a part of

our regular routine rather than an exception.

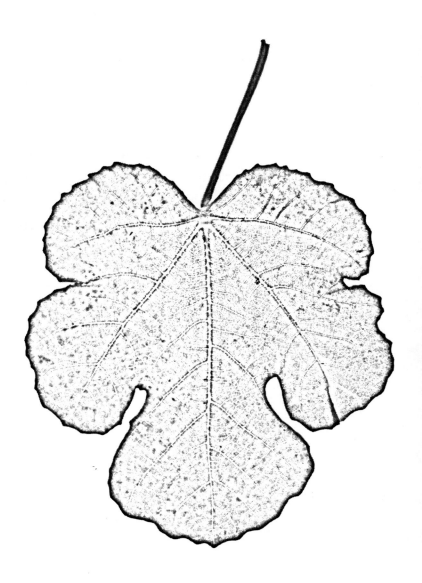

CHAPTER 3

SOOTHE THOSE FRAZZLED NERVES

We said in the last chapter that breath is a direct pathway to our nervous system, and that conscious breath can restore our sense of ease and relaxation. Unhindered breathing results in a sense of well-being, whereas stress impedes our breathing, and chronic stress often leads to the formation of shallow breathing patterns that can increase anxiety or diminish our sense of vitality.

Our senses—sight, touch, hearing, smell, and taste—are also pathways to our nervous system. These mechanisms tell us what is good for us and what is not, what we should approach or avoid. When our senses are constantly stimulated, they become numb and no longer serve us effectively. Like the frog mentioned in Chapter 1, our ability to choose the right course of action for ourselves can be dangerously diminished.

This chapter discusses the delicate relationship we have with the world around us, and how a fast-paced lifestyle can dull our senses. Once we understand how our nervous system interacts with our surroundings, it will be easy to see the necessity of protecting ourselves from too much stimulation. With awareness and intention, we can reduce stimuli in a manner that does not compromise our daily functioning. An awareness exercise is included to enhance our understanding, and exercises at the end of the chapter provide effective ways to refresh our senses.

ENERGY EXCHANGE

Despite appearances to the contrary, we are not solid entities insulated from the rest of the universe. Yoga and Ayurveda, two sister sciences that evolved from the same philosophical roots, teach that all of life rises from a common energy source. This view is supported by modern physics, which teaches that everything, including us, is composed of groups of molecules moving in space, propelled by energy. From this perspective, the universe can be seen as an ecosystem in which any change or action affects the whole. Since we are part of this ecosystem, our boundaries are permeable rather than solid, and we are more vulnerable to our surroundings than we might think. We absorb the energies from what is around us. In turn, all we do, think, and feel affects everything else, whether or not the effects are immediately apparent. This reciprocal process generally takes place on subtle levels and beyond our normal range of perception.

We have all experienced energy exchange with our environment, even though we may not have identified these experiences as such. When our living or work spaces become cluttered and disorganized, for example, we might experience disquiet and find it difficult to concentrate. Similarly, it is not unusual for our mood to be affected by the noise level or colors of our surroundings. The desert, ocean, and mountains are settings with very different energetic effects. Depending on our own energetic composition, many of us have a special affinity to one of these landscapes and experience a sense of renewal when we are in that setting.

People around us are a part of our environment, and the energies they project affect us. We know this intuitively when we say that someone brings out the best in us. There are also people who leave us feeling worse. We say that certain people "bore us," meaning that we experience their energy as being heavy and dull. We might be able to tolerate some people for only short periods of time, since being around them leaves us feeling agitated and irritable.

Because this energy exchange is a subtle process that we can neither see nor touch, many people expose themselves to a great deal of stress without comprehending that they are doing so. Far too many women, for example, excuse their partner's abusive behavior on the grounds that they were not physically struck. Yet the energy generated by loud, angry shouting, or shattering glass, as objects are thrown in anger, touches us in the subtler dimensions of our being. Similarly, children are affected energetically by violence in the home, whether or not they are the objects of direct physical abuse.

Another example of this interpersonal energy exchange is illustrated by the saying, "One bad apple spoils the whole barrel." When I worked for a community mental health center, I served as a field supervisor for graduate social work interns. One year I had the pleasure of training three delightful young women, all bright and eager to learn. We had stimulating supervision meetings, bonded closely, and collaborated well. Mid-year a fourth student, who was highly competitive, transferred into our group. The energy changed almost instantly, and our wonderful sense of camaraderie promptly dissipated. This happened spontaneously at an instinctual level, before anyone could intellectually identify that the atmosphere was different.

On an even subtler level, studies have shown that women who live together become synchronized energetically and eventually all menstruate around the same time each month; grandfather clocks placed in the same room will, in time, tick in unison. Vastu Shastra and Feng Shui, ancient energy-based sciences, teach that the orientation of a building, the directional axis of rooms, the placement of furniture, and the colors we surround ourselves with all directly influence us through their energy vibrations, affecting our sleep, our concentration, and our emotions.

SENSORY OVERLOAD

Whereas insects negotiate their environment with antennas, humans manage with five senses: sight, hearing, taste, smell, and touch. Damage the antenna of a cricket and its functioning is impaired. Similarly, damage to just one of our senses seriously affects our overall functioning. We all need a certain amount of healthy stimulation to retain a sense of novelty and keep our lives interesting. Too much stimulation, or the wrong kind, however, dulls our senses, impairs their functioning, and irritates the nervous system. To become more aware of how our senses can be influenced by different stimuli, take a little time to engage in the following awareness exercise.

AWARENESS EXERCISE

Sit quietly and take a few conscious breaths to center yourself. Now imagine fully each of the following scenarios, taking a short breathing break between each one and noticing how you are affected.

- Listening to your favorite sonata
- Hearing a power lawn mower
- Viewing an Impressionist painting
- Looking at photographs of Holocaust victims
- Tasting your favorite dessert
- Sucking on a lemon
- Feeling soft flannel against your skin
- Falling down and scraping your knee
- Smelling your favorite incense
- Smelling garbage

Each of these experiences, though they are only imagined, affects you differently. We can all recall our senses being aggravated by excessive stimuli, such as loud noises, blinding lights, putrid smells, freezing cold, or bitter-tasting foods. Imagine these stimuli being frequent or ongoing, and it is not difficult to see how they might eventually be too much for our senses, and in turn for our nervous system.

Whether or not we notice, we suffer from overstimulation in a variety of ways. For example, we are overloaded by information. News from all corners of the world, sometimes with traumatizing details, is broadcasted continuously. Ads pop up on computer screens uninvited, telemarketers intrude into the privacy of our homes, and a staggering amount of junk mail arrives daily. While technological advances have greatly eased our lives, they also create other problems. Cell phones, for example, can be overused, leaving us with less quiet time for renewing our senses. Staying in touch with work by phone or computer while away from the office means our already excessively long workdays become even longer. We talk on the cell phone wile we drive, walk, or eat. This multi-tasking is extremely taxing on the nervous system.

All of these factors contribute to an environment in which our senses are almost constantly bombarded. Possibly as the result of this gradual dulling of our senses, many things, including music, movies, media presentations, fashion, and even toys, have become louder, brighter, harsher, faster, and brasher. It seems as though we are caught in a vicious cycle of overstimulation that leads to the dulling of our senses, to our turning up the volume, to the further dulling of our senses, to our turning up the volume even higher. It is important to break this cycle because frayed nerves need the volume turned down, not up, for chronic overstimulation serves like a slow-acting toxin. This is a serious problem that is not being adequately or appropriately addressed.

TRUSTING OUR INNER EXPERIENCE

When it comes to keeping our nervous system calm, it is crucial to be in touch with how we are influenced by the sights, sounds, and smells around us and by the people with whom we spend time. This requires that we not only keep our senses refreshed so they can receive and process stimuli accurately, but also that we trust the information they give us. Regardless of what other people or our unexamined beliefs tell us about how we should respond to someone or something, our internal reactions are our only valid guide in this matter. Far too often we doubt our inner experiences and struggle against them, adding insult to injury. This stress-inducing pattern of second-guessing ourselves leaves us forever uncertain.

When I counsel parents, I recommend strongly that they avoid negating their children's experiences, because the ability to trust the cues we receive from our senses is an essential skill for moving through life effectively. There is a difference between managing the behavior of children and overriding their experiences. We can, for example, encourage them to try new foods without having to persuade them they like the taste. We can ask them to put on a jacket without having to convince them that they feel cold. Similarly, we can allow them to not like a relative or family friend and then negotiate with them a respectful way to behave toward that person. We can even use these occasions to teach them to distinguish between sensory functions, such as differentiating between not liking the appearance of a food and not liking its actual taste.

These same guidelines can be applied to our own responses to inner experiences. We can acknowledge and honor what we feel and let go of our judgments, turning our attention to understanding ourselves better by impartially observing our experiences. When we spend time with people or in activities that affect us negatively, for example, we can observe our experience and take an interest in finding out what it is about the experience that affects us in this manner. This process of impartial observation is referred to as self-inquiry in yoga, and it is a recommended practice that we will discuss in more detail in Chapter 6. I have found that when I take some space and time to tune in and observe, a better understanding of myself and my relationship to the situation invariably emerges.

Validation for trusting our senses is in short supply in our society, where greater validity is accorded to external authority—such as research, experts, and literature—than to inner experiences. Far too often and to our detriment, we ignore what our body tells us in favor of expert opinions. Ken, for example, was given a new medication that had severely negative side effects for him. He returned to his physician with the intention of asking for a different prescription, since there were a variety of medications on the market for his particular problem. However, his physician doubled his dosage and Ken agreed. His symptoms became even worse, and the residual side effects lasted a long time, even after he finally took himself off the medication.

Healing practices such as yoga and meditation, when taught properly, are excellent ways to reconnect with our internal experiences because they emphasize an internal focus. When my yoga students ask me where they should feel a certain stretch, I always ask them to tell me where they actually feel it in their body. This is not to avoid answering them, but to reinforce the message that they are the experts of their own experiences. Even though reconnecting with inner experiences is generally not the primary reason most people come to yoga and meditation, it is nevertheless one of the factors that make these practices so effective for relieving stress and enhancing creativity.

DRAWING THE SENSES INWARD

In our society yoga has become associated with the stretching and toning of our physical body. Other important yogic practices, such as the intentional withdrawal of our senses from stimuli, are less emphasized. This quieting of the senses is an essential ingredient in all healing arts known for their efficacy in reducing stress, including yoga, meditation, massage, and Qigong. All these practices help us to become quiet, still, and inwardly focused, allowing stimuli to fade into the background of our consciousness.

The relaxation period at the end of a yoga class is an excellent example of the withdrawal of our senses. We lie down in a quiet place to help us withdraw our sense of hearing from our environment. We close our eyes, perhaps even put on an eye pillow, to withdraw our sense of sight. We become completely still to withdraw our kinesthetic senses. We focus our attention inward and slowly allow our minds to become quiet. Withdrawing our senses in these ways helps to transport us into a different state of consciousness, wherein we are completely relaxed but at the same time fully awake and aware. In fact, the structure of a properly sequenced yoga class, in its fine balance between activity and stillness and in its attention to transitions, can serve as an excellent model for a healthy, balanced lifestyle.

Besides relieving stress, regularly drawing our senses inward and quieting the nervous system also increases our intuition and creativity. Artists confirm that spending quiet time in solitude is one of the essential conditions for allowing creativity to flow. Consider the possibility that we are all born with unlimited potential for intuition and creativity, and that it is the dulling of our senses that blocks us from reaching our fullest potential.

REDUCING STIMULATION

We can reduce the stimulation in our lives in many ways, without having to surrender the conveniences offered by useful technology, so long as we practice moderation and judicious usage. For example, we can be selective as to when we turn on our TV, cell phone, and radio, remembering that they are for our convenience, not the other way around. If the TV is being left on for background noise, ask yourself why that is necessary, and what feeling states you might be trying to avoid through the noise. What is it about silence that we need to keep it a stranger? Likewise, constant cell phone interruptions keep us at others' beck and call. It is important to remember we are setting the stage for chronic stress when we allow work to creep into our off-hours.

We can give our senses short rests throughout the day. We can reduce multi-tasking, eat an occasional meal in contemplative silence, or spend more leisure time quietly in nature. We can give ourselves adequate transition time between tasks so we don't rush. We can choose to spend less time around people who influence us negatively, or spend that time with them differently. We can take lunch breaks, days off, quiet, restful weekends, or regular vacations. We can choose low-stimuli leisure activities such as hiking or kayaking instead of high-stimuli destinations like Disneyland and Las Vegas. Above all, we can choose to simplify our lives and be clear about our priorities so that we don't wear ourselves out through sensory overload.

THE IMPORTANCE OF REST

Americans work more hours than people in any other developed nation. We take an average of ten vacation days a year. The minimum annual vacation for Europeans is five or more weeks, and many French enjoy vacations of two months. This is a topic that invariably comes up when I meet Europeans during my travels. They find our workaholic tendencies incomprehensible. Frequently it is not a matter of our not having vacation time available to us, but a choice to not take all the vacation time we are allotted. In addition to overstimulating the senses, working nonstop has serious health consequences. A study showed that men who took annual vacations were less likely to die of heart disease, one of the leading causes of death in our society.

It is not unusual for people to mistakenly dismiss quiet time as unproductive time, not understanding that our bodies and minds need time for renewal the same way our cars need periodic tuneups. During our periods of rest, repair and restoration takes place physically, mentally, and spiritually. It is easy to get caught up in the moment and fret about things that, in the larger scheme of things, are relatively unimportant.

You might feel mildly anxious when you begin to slow down. This is not unusual for people who have become used to a fast-paced rhythm. Your gauge of what is normal needs readjustment. Remind yourself that change is always a little uncomfortable, especially in the beginning, that you are doing what is necessary to improve the quality of your life. Remember that frequently we work more efficiently and the quality of our work improves when we are rested and clear headed. The following exercise will help you continue the work you have started by supporting your breath and helping you relax.

EXERCISE 3—Breath with Movement

Synchronizing our breath with gentle movements soothes the nervous system while gently stretching tense muscles and lubricating the joints, both of which are sites where tension accumulates. This process also helps us draw our senses away from external stimuli and focus instead on our breath and internal experience. Remember the parameters for practice from the last chapter and set aside a sufficient amount of time for yourself, be in a quiet place, and forestall interruptions. Soothing, rhythmic music will be particularly enhancing for this exercise, as will an eye pillow filled with flax seeds for the final relaxation. Remember the option of recording the instructions so you can play them back for yourself.

Breathe through the nose and allow your breath to be long and easy, and your movements slow and light, as though they were fueled by the breath rather than your muscles. If you find that you need to take more than one breath to complete a movement, allow that to happen and simply pause in the middle of the movement. At no time should you force or hold your breath.

1. Lie comfortably on your back on the floor, with your arms by your sides. If you experience strain in your lower back, use a cushion or rolled-up blanket under your knees for support. If your chin tilts up, place a folded blanket or towel under your head so that your neck can be extended naturally, with its normal curve intact.

2. Tune in to your breathing and allow your body to relax. Notice that there are four parts to your breath: the inhalation, followed by a pause, then the exhalation, followed by a pause. Continue to lie here, breathe, and notice this pattern for three to four minutes.

3. When you next inhale, allow your arms to slowly rise toward the floor over your head, as though being lifted by your breath. Face the palms of your hands toward each other and reach all the way to the floor if you can, then pause in your movement during

the pause in your breath, stretching your whole body by extending through your feet if that is comfortable for you. When you exhale, allow your exhalation to lower your arms back down to your sides, again pausing in your movement when your breath pauses. Repeat this three more times, focusing your attention on synchronizing your movements with your breath, on allowing the breath to initiate the movements, and on making the movements as light and effortless as possible. When you are finished, rest with your arms by your sides and pay attention to the four parts of your breath for a few rounds of breathing.

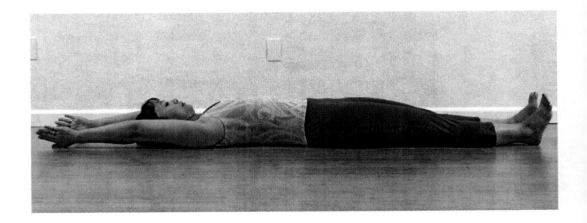

4. Once again, raise your arms overhead toward the floor when you inhale. Pause when your breath pauses. When you exhale, bend your right knee and bring it toward your chest while you lower your arms and hug your right shin toward the chest and extend your left leg along the floor, pressing through the heel. Pause when your breath pauses. On the next inhalation, float your arms overhead and your right leg back down to the floor. Now repeat the sequence with your left leg. Repeat the whole sequence on each side three times. When you are finished, rest for a few breaths with your arms by your sides.

5. Now bend your knees and place your feet on the floor, in line with your sitting bones, with your toes pointing straight ahead. When you next inhale, press into your feet evenly to help your hips lift toward the ceiling as your arms again rise toward the floor over your head. Extend your spine away from you as you lift to make space in the lower back; at the same time broaden across your collarbones and come toward the top of your shoulders. When you exhale, release your torso down, vertebrae by vertebrae, as you bring your arms back down to your sides. Honor the pauses between your inhalations and exhalations by pausing accordingly

in your movements. Do this three more times, then bring your knees toward your chest and hug your shins with your arms as you rest for a few breaths, rocking gently from side to side to massage your sacrum and lower back if the rocking feels good.

6. With your knees in toward your chest, when you next inhale, extend your feet toward the ceiling by straightening your legs and stretching through the heels while you lift your arms overhead toward the floor. Feel your whole body lengthen. When you exhale, bend your knees toward your chest and lower your arms to hug your shins. Pause in your movements when your breath pauses. Do this three more times and then rest for a few breaths while you hug your shins toward your chest. Turn over to your left side.

7. Keep your knees bent and together in a fetal position, with your arms straight out in front of your chest, hands together. On the next inhalation, keep your left shoulder on the floor, the knees together,

and your eyes on your right hand as it moves in an arc toward the floor behind you. Your right hand may or may not actually touch the floor behind you. Your body will now be in a twisted position. On your exhalation, return to the original position, arms extended and hands together. Repeat this three more times, then stay in the twisted position. Bend your right elbow and rest your forearm on your right hip and take five slow breaths before returning to the original position. Repeat this sequence lying on your right side.

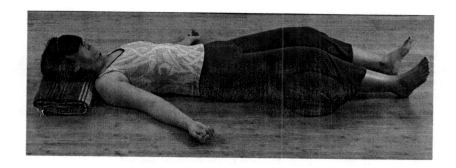

8. Finally, rest on your back and relax your body onto the ground. Pay attention to your breathing and notice the inhalation, exhalation, and pauses. Allow the breath to become smooth and the exhalation to become longer than the inhalation. Allow the exhalation to be as long as it wants to be, until your body decides to inhale again. Do not force the breath in any manner. Work with it gently, allowing it to take the lead. Breathe this way for one to two minutes, then allow your breath to be normal for a few rounds. Close your eyes and place an eye pillow over them if you decide to use one. Make sure you are comfortable. Imagine that you are getting heavier and heavier as you exhale. Rest quietly this way for at least five to ten minutes.

EXERCISE 4—Relaxing Upside Down

For the following exercise, a yoga bolster is the ideal firm support for your pelvis. I recommend that you invest in one if you plan to continue this practice, since it is difficult to duplicate the way a bolster supports your body, and being supported properly helps the body to truly relax. Being properly equipped is part of good self-care. In the absence of a bolster, substitute two firm Mexican blankets or three to four bath towels folded as described below. An eye pillow filled with flax seed and placed over the eyes reduces rapid eye movement, supports the drawing of your senses inward, and enhances your relaxation.

Because your pelvis is elevated in this pose, your internal organs become suspended upside down. They are stimulated in a beneficial way even as you rest. Your heart also works less than when it has to pump the blood back up from your legs. This pose is deeply relaxing and over time can lower blood pressure. However, if you suffer from heart disease, glaucoma, uncontrolled hypertension, or if you are menstruating, do not elevate your pelvis, just rest it flat on the floor.

1. Fold three bath towels in thirds lengthwise, then fold the long strips in half. Stack the rectangles on top of each other. Place this stack of folded towels with the long side against the wall, approximately two inches away from it.

2. Bend your knees and rest your left hip on the left edge of the stack of towels and your buttocks against the wall.

3. Swing your legs up the wall so that the back of your pelvis rests in the middle of the stack of towels. If your hamstrings permit,

your buttocks and the backs of your legs should be against the wall. This requires a little practice, since our body tends to come away from the wall as we swing our legs up. If you have very tight hamstrings, your buttocks and the backs of your legs may need to be an inch or two away from the wall.

4.   Your mid- and upper back should be on the floor. Press your upper arms against the floor so you can feel your shoulder blades move into the back of your body, opening your chest. Now relax, with your eye pillow over your eyes, if you are using one, and your arms bent upward in an "I surrender" position. If you feel strain in your lower back, reduce the number of towels. If necessary, use no elevation and lie directly on the floor with your legs up the wall.

5.   Stay here for five to ten minutes, breathing slowly and allowing your body to release into the support of the towels and your mind to quiet.

EXERCISE 5—Reclining Cobbler's Pose

For this restorative pose, use the same type of support as in the last exercise, plus three more towels or blankets to support your head and thighs. Again, a yoga bolster will provide the optimum support for your body and an eye pillow will enhance relaxation. This pose passively opens the pelvis and abdominal region and is therefore particularly good during menstruation or menopause, and aids digestion. It is also good for headaches, especially if an additional eye pillow can be placed on the forehead, or if the eyes can be very loosely wrapped with an elastic bandage.

1.   Have a bolster or fold three towels, stacking them as in Exercise 4. Fold another towel in thirds lengthwise, then in thirds again so that it forms a shorter rectangle. Place this crosswise at one end of the stack of towels to serve as a pillow. We will refer to this end as the "top." Fold two more towels in thirds lengthwise, roll them up, and keep them handy.

2. Sit with your back facing the bolster or towels at the "bottom" end of the stack and slowly lower your torso onto the support, centering yourself on the bolster or folded towels. Keeping your knees bent, step into both feet, lift your buttocks, and use your hands to move the buttock flesh toward your feet before setting your pelvis back down. This creates more space in your lower back.

3. Now put the soles of your feet together and allow your knees to relax away from the center and toward the floor. Place a rolled towel under each thigh for support and to avoid straining or stretching the inner thighs. Lie down on the bolster or folded towels and place your head on the "pillow." If your chin tilts up toward the ceiling, increase the height of the support under your head. Press your elbows against the floor to lift and open your chest before relaxing your body onto the bolster or towels completely.

4. Close your eyes and place your eye pillow over them. Breathe softly and rest here for five to ten minutes.

SUMMARY

Our senses are like antennas for deciphering the world around us. Overstimulation leads to stress and has the tendency to dull our senses, overwhelm our nervous system, and impair our general functioning. Because we are essentially composed of energy, we are vulnerable to our environment. Our boundaries are permeable, we are affected by all that is around us, and in turn we affect all there is through our thoughts, feelings, and actions.

It is essential for us to protect ourselves from sensory toxins and rejuvenate our sensory organs regularly. Some of the ways we can accomplish this include selectively limiting stimuli, drawing our senses inward, breathing consciously, and resting quietly. Caring for ourselves in our increasingly complex world requires knowledge, skill, discernment, intention, and discipline. When we make self-care a priority, we are more than amply rewarded by a sense of contentment and satisfaction that wealth and material possessions cannot bring us. &

The capacity to experience a full range of emotions

is an integral part of being human.

CHAPTER 4

POSITIVE WAYS WITH NEGATIVE FEELINGS

*W*e said in the last chapter that we are made up of energy. Our boundaries are permeable, so we are sensitive to what is around us; our five senses receive and process input from our environment. We now take these concepts a step further. As the environment stimulates our senses, sensations are triggered, some of which we experience as feelings. We refer to feelings as emotions when they are complex.

The ability to manage our emotions constructively is crucial to reducing stress. If we do not pause and reflect long enough to understand what we are feeling and why, we do not know how to respond appropriately. Wisdom traditions refer to the part of our consciousness that impartially observes our feelings as the "Inner Witness." When we lack this awareness, we are likely to mismanage our feelings and make things worse, thus creating more stress for ourselves.

This chapter discusses the nature of feelings, some consequences of not managing them constructively, and the difference between feelings and behavior. We discuss the phenomenon of blocked energy and identify some of the ways these blockages can interfere with our daily functioning. We look at common patterns that tend to develop as a result of habitually avoiding our emotions, how they might be manifested, and why they are harmful to our physical and emotional health. Finally, we explore conscious breathing, meditation, and journaling as vehicles for enhancing our ability to pause and reflect.

THE NATURE OF EMOTIONS

Our five senses receive input from the environment, and feelings are one form of energy generated by this interaction. Like all energy, feelings have their own momentum and seek expression. They follow an arching rhythm that escalates to a climax then de-escalates, finally subsiding in resolution. The intensity and duration of feelings depend on the magnitude of the stimuli and our unique vulnerability to it. Our language recognizes the energetic basis for feelings when we say that certain situations or people hold a special "charge" for us or that we could feel emotions "welling up." I still remember my first lucid experience of anger. It began as the sensation of expanding energy in my chest, filling my chest cavity and moving into my arms and legs. I could feel the energy as heat in my face, fullness in the region of my chest, and tingling in my hands. Then, slowly, the energy subsided. The experience was clean and clear cut. I knew that I felt furious because I felt offended by what had happened, but I also felt totally centered within myself and without any need to take action. This was a particularly memorable moment for me because my habitual response when I felt offended had always been to short-circuit the process by prematurely releasing the energy through angry outbursts that I would subsequently regret.

Because feelings are energy seeking resolution, they are transient when not interfered with. We can see the transient nature of feelings by observing young children whose thinking function has not yet fully developed and who have not yet been taught to censor themselves. Their feelings are totally in the foreground of their experience. A two year old, for example, can easily go through frustration, excitement, joy, and heartbreak within the span of only a few moments and retain very little memory of these emotions once they pass.

FEELINGS ARE NEITHER GOOD NOR BAD

Nearly every culture and subculture has built a value system around feelings, valuing certain feelings above others. A spiritual community, for example, might prioritize emotions such as compassion and love. A street gang, on the other hand, is more likely to look down on these same emotions. Instead, they might esteem anger, disdain, and vengefulness.

As a result of our biases about feelings, we tend to dichotomize them into good and bad, right and wrong. In doing so, we create confusion: feelings are simply energy and therefore without moral significance, a natural and universal phenomenon. The capacity to experience the full range of emotions is an integral part of being human. It is not possible for us to choose which feelings we will and will not experience without repercussions. Separating feelings into categories according to their desirability creates a situation in which we are likely to judge ourselves for our natural responses and to set expectations for ourselves that are impossible to fulfill. Such a situation interferes with the natural resolution of emotional energy and creates self-induced stress.

NOT ALL FEELINGS ARE CONSTRUCTIVE

Although feelings have no moral significance, not all feelings are equally constructive for our well-being. Certain feelings, such as anger, resentment, impatience, hatred, rage, and antagonism, are likely to trigger the stress response. These feelings tend to build heat in the body. The English language reflects this phenomenon in that someone with a bad temper is considered "hot-headed." When these feelings are frequent or chronic, they tend to elevate blood pressure, increase the heart rate, and take their toll on our health.

Since these feelings are part of the human experience and therefore not always avoidable, the best way to manage them in the moment is by engaging in the conscious rhythmic breathing discussed later in this chapter. By observing our breathing and experiencing the movement of the breath in our body, we not only give ourselves the support to tolerate these feelings as they traverse their natural course toward resolution, but we also activate our relaxation response, which restores homeostasis to our physiology. Over time, practicing conscious breathing under these circumstances cultivates our Witness Consciousness, which plays a significant role in reducing our overall stress.

DISTINGUISHING FEELINGS FROM BEHAVIOR

While feelings are neutral and not subject to judgment, behavior is another matter. Feeling angry is an internal experience and not the same as striking out in anger through actions or words. This is a distinction that is commonly misunderstood. I have counseled people who mistakenly believed that their emotions justified behaviors that escalated their difficulties. Sam, for example, felt he had the right to raise his voice when he felt irritated by Sue. Mindy, on the other hand, felt justified to stop speaking to Doug when he forgot her birthday and she felt hurt. It takes work to come to the understanding that while we cannot control our emotions, we are totally responsible for our behavior.

When the expression of feelings is encouraged during the course of psychotherapy, we are referring to the experiencing and identifying of what we are feeling, not to angry outbursts. This process of experiencing and identifying is similar to the process of noting our feelings and thoughts in mindfulness meditation. Both are stress-reducing mediums that help us modulate our emotions and reduce our reactivity.

Learning to manage my feelings was a major undertaking for me. I was known for my quick temper in my younger years. Feelings, especially those of anger, hurt, or fear, would overwhelm me until I discharged the tension through angry outbursts. Those outbursts not only left me in a bad light but also harmed my relationships as well as my self-esteem. It was not until I came to yoga and meditation that my ability to contain my emotions improved. It still seems a miracle that I can now behave in a manner that allows me to feel good about myself, despite strong negative emotions.

RELATING TO EMOTIONS CONSTRUCTIVELY

While there are no bad feelings, certain feelings are more unpleasant than others. We might be frightened by unfamiliar feelings or by the intensity of some feelings. These factors, in addition to our inclination to judge certain feelings, result in a tendency to avoid them. In general, our culture tends to shy away from feelings that increase our sense of vulnerability, such as hurt, shame, envy, guilt, or fear.

Wisdom traditions teach that human suffering is the result of our attempts to avoid what is unavoidable and to cling to what cannot last. This teaching is as applicable to how we relate to our emotions as it is to all other aspects of living. Certain unpleasant experiences are a natural and unavoidable part of life. We age, we sometimes fall short of our expectations, we lose people we love, and we experience changes whether we welcome them or not. Attempts to avoid the feelings that are evoked by these experiences work against the natural process. Not only can we not succeed, but we are also likely to create even more difficulties for ourselves. The extreme avoidance of uncomfortable feelings, for example, is one of the primary dynamics behind agoraphobia.

Like unpleasant experiences, the pleasurable ones are also transient in nature. Attempts to make all our experiences pleasurable or to unduly prolong pleasurable sensations are also against the natural order and cannot succeed. This avoidance of pain and clinging to pleasure is the dynamic behind addiction, whether it be to food, alcohol, drugs, sex, gambling, or shopping. It is far more constructive to understand and accept the nature of feelings and the life process itself, and to develop the skills to manage our emotions.

PATTERNS OF AVOIDANCE

A common way to avoid feelings is by distracting ourselves. Rather than feeling lonely, hurt, or disappointed, we might drink too much, eat too much, or involve ourselves in destructive relationships. Long hours in front of the TV or electronic games can similarly numb us from many emotions. A pattern of working long hours followed by crashing in front of the TV or the computer has become more and more common in our workaholic society. Should this happen to be one of your patterns, consider the possibility of spending an evening in a more contemplative manner, perhaps taking a walk or sitting quietly in the garden, and find out what you might have been trying to avoid.

Because our culture has difficulties contending with the more vulnerable feelings of hurt, shame, envy, guilt, and fear, one way we avoid these feelings is by veering into anger, a secondary emotion that serves as a cover-up for them. We might become angry with ourselves or with others. To explore this process experientially, remember the last few times you were angry, and look a little deeper to see whether one of these more vulnerable feelings might have been lurking beneath the anger.

We can also bypass frustration or disappointment by blaming and finding fault with ourselves or others. Unfortunately, bypassing feelings through anger or blame is not in our best interests, since both of these avenues are far more likely to elicit a more hostile and less conciliatory response from the other person than hurt, shame, fear, or disappointment, and our self-esteem suffers from self-blame.

Another way to avoid feelings is to push them out of our awareness. When this pattern of avoidance becomes habitual, we become emotionally numb and out of touch with our inner life. Ed, a successful businessman in his middle forties, had a stressful childhood. His mother suffered from severe depression in an era that lacked the sophisticated antidepressant medications we have today. Being the oldest, Ed assumed adult responsibilities prematurely. He learned to keep his feelings at bay in order to take care of the tasks at hand. By adulthood Ed had largely lost his ability to experience gradations of feelings, and he continued to avoid feelings by routinely refusing to acknowledge or discuss any subjects that might be potentially emotional. As a result, Ed's intimate relationships suffered. His first wife left him after five years of marriage, complaining they lacked intimacy. Ed sought psychotherapy when his second wife began voicing similar complaints.

FEELINGS AND DECISION MAKING

Our culture tends to over-value external dictates and the rational process and under-value the subjective and intuitive. While many decisions can be made objectively, this is not the best process for making decisions affecting matters close to our heart. Because feelings arise as a result of our senses interacting with the external world against the background of our inherent constitution, they provide us with important information. Just as we need to consider the weather pattern in addition to a compass when we sail the oceans, we need to be in tune with our emotions as well as our intellect to make optimally beneficial life decisions. If we want work that we are passionate about, relationships that are inherently satisfying and fulfilling, a home in which we feel safe and cozy, the rational process will get us only half the distance.

As an example, I have lived in many houses. I never chose them for rational reasons alone, such as the resale value or projections about the neighborhood. Those factors mattered, but I also needed the house to *feel* right. I have tried to identify the criteria for this feeling, such as the house having lots of sunlight, nicely proportioned rooms, or a coherent floor plan. In actuality, however, the *feel* of the place transcends all of those parts for me. I have been the same way with my work. Job security, retirement benefits, prestige, or the amount that I earn was not a sufficient incentive for me unless I also experienced a high degree of interest in my daily tasks and felt comfortable with the values and goals of my employer.

The point here is not that my way is the right way, but I do believe that many of us will find more satisfaction in life if we allow ourselves to give more credence to our feeling and intuitive functions. Furthermore, it is only through an intimate relationship with our emotions that we can digest and integrate our life experiences and learn from them.

Pat was referred to me by her physician for stress. She was a highly intellectual woman who tended to think her way through life decisions, relying almost exclusively on reason, logic, and external factors. This meant that while many of her decisions might have been right from a rational point of view, they were actually not personally suitable for her. For example, Pat became a trial attorney because it was a prestigious and lucrative profession. Unfortunately, Pat abhorred conflict and found trial work extremely stressful. Pat also served on several boards and committees to promote herself professionally. This only added to her distress, since she had a constitution that needed quiet time alone to rejuvenate. Instead of listening to her inner experiences, Pat judged herself harshly for her feelings, a process that increased her level of stress.

On a more concrete level, avoiding feelings truncates our experience and disrupts the natural flow of emotional energy. Like a pressure cooker that has the potential of blowing its lid when too much steam has built up, pent-up emotional energy can also reach explosive levels. Angry outbursts, self-destructive behaviors, hypertension, inflammatory conditions, chronic headaches, and hives and other skin eruptions can take on an entirely different meaning when considered from this perspective. Since it takes a tremendous amount of energy to keep emotions repressed, this state of mind can also contribute to conditions like fatigue, lethargy, depression, or emotional numbness.

CHANGE AND SELF-ACCEPTANCE
Habitual patterns can be unlearned through intention, focused awareness, and most importantly, a self-accepting attitude. Ed, for example, learned to become aware of the muscular tension that he used to suppress his feelings. By learning to gradually relax his muscles, he began to slowly experience the suppressed sensations and associate them with various feelings.

Gestalt Therapy refers to these patterns as "creative adaptations." They were, once upon a time, effective solutions for specific problems we faced. It was only when they faded from our awareness and became our generalized responses to all situations that they became no longer suitable or adaptive. As we reverse old patterns, it is important to remember that they rose out of our creativity and resilience at some past time. As we have said before, a compassionate and loving attitude toward ourselves is a prerequisite for constructive change.

VEHICLES FOR CHANGE

To manage our feelings, especially the ones we tend to avoid, we must be able to sustain ourselves through the intensity of their energetic expression. Conscious breathing, journaling, and meditation are three effective tools we can use for this purpose. Routinely practicing these methods with less intense emotions will incorporate them into our repertoire and prepare us for more difficult emotions that are bound to arise. Besides facilitating the passage of difficult emotions, these practices also enhance our emotional and spiritual growth.

CONSCIOUS BREATHING

When we are overtaken by strong, difficult-to-tolerate emotions, the best remedy is to give ourselves plenty of time, become still, and tune in to the rhythm of our breathing. Avoid acting in the heat of emotion. Instead, feel the sensations of the breath entering the nostrils, the body filling and emptying as we breathe, the way the breath moves though our body. It is important to avoid engaging our thinking function, since thinking about these sensations disrupts the energy flow. Simply persist so the energy can move through us toward a natural resolution. Lying down in a place where we feel safe and making ourselves warm and as physically comfortable as possible can help to facilitate the process.

Each of us experiences the flow of energy differently. Rage, for example, might be experienced as a tightening of the jaw, a clenching of the hands, or a fullness in the chest; hurt as a stabbing pain in the chest or an emptiness in our heart; anxiety as fluttering in the chest or tightness in the throat; and fear as a tight, compressed ball of energy in the pit of our stomach or a sense of unreality. We can sustain ourselves by allowing these experiences to run their courses as we modulate our breathing to accommodate them. We might even moan to support painful feelings, even curl up physically into a ball.

This is a difficult practice, one that requires persistence before it begins to feel natural. It is, however, well worth the struggle. It is through such a practice that we strengthen our immunity to stress. We also gain a tremendous sense of self-sufficiency and confidence from knowing we can sustain ourselves through the most difficult emotions, and our sense of our place in the world becomes altered for the better. The following is a personal example.

Having had an extraordinarily stressful childhood, I did not learn adequate self-soothing skills and always depended on other people for emotional support. A pivotal moment that changed all this came when I went through the end of a relationship. Instead of calling my friends for support, I went to bed for an entire afternoon. I breathed consciously and allowed myself the experience of my feelings, observing the process all the while. Slowly, the realization came to me that I was separate from those feelings; that I, the observer, was far more spacious than the transient feelings and that there was nothing to fear. Most importantly, a sense of strength and resiliency slowly spread through me along with a knowing that I could survive any experience life had in store for me, including that of being entirely alone.

JOURNALING

Writing down our feelings is another way we can support ourselves through strong emotions. Journaling is used in many programs geared toward healing, growth, or creativity. It is, for example, an integral part of twelve-step recovery programs. It is the "morning pages" in *The Artist's Way*, used as a daily practice to enhance creativity. Journaling helps us manage our emotions in a variety of ways. Writing creates a grounding effect by anchoring the feelings onto the pages and providing us with a means of tempering those feelings until we can gradually put things into perspective. People frequently feel lighter after they journal, as though they have dropped a weight off their shoulders. Sometimes when emotions are particularly strong or complex, we may have to journal repeatedly about the same event over the span of several days before experiencing clarity or relief. Recent research has found that journaling about our feelings after traumatic events enhances general health and promotes recovery from chronic illnesses.

Journaling is different from writing in a diary. Diaries record events. In journaling we write down our feelings and reactions to selected events that are emotionally affecting us, and we glean new information about ourselves as a result of these experiences and journaling. When we journal, it is important to write without regard to grammar, sentence structure, or any of the rules about composition we were taught. This way of writing can be difficult, especially for those of us with perfectionist tendencies, but it is important, since thinking about grammar and sentence structure interrupts the emotional flow. Journals are private, not written for anyone else to read. Frequently we don't even reread what we have written.

Do not try to be logical, articulate, or intellectual. Instead, imagine your pen as an extension of your heart, and write down whatever is there, without censorship. You can write about the wave-like energy of your emotions, describing the sensations and any images that might form, or any associations and memories that might surface, again just putting the words down without intellectual analysis. To feel safe in writing in an uncensored way, it is crucial that no one reads your journal. Keeping your journal in a safe place is important. Since the purpose of journaling is to unload feelings, not to keep a record of them, many people do not keep their journals for any length of time.

To reduce stress, start a daily practice of journaling, writing down your feelings about one or two significant events that have recently affected you. These don't have to be negative events. Your joy as you watched your child sleep, for example, or your experience sitting on your patio and watching the sun set are also worthy topics for journaling. As with any practice, it is important to set aside a regular time for your journaling, even though it might be only ten to fifteen minutes. You can reduce the frequency of journaling once you feel you understand the process. The goal is to develop a familiar tool you can use to manage your feelings when under stress. Many people enjoy this intimate time with themselves so much that they continue to journal regularly.

LETTERS WE DON'T SEND

Writing letters we don't send is a form of journaling that is particularly effective for managing difficult feelings toward people who are important to us, whether or not they are currently in our lives. We write the letter as though we were talking directly to the person in a face-to-face conversation. Since the letter will not be sent, we write whatever we feel, holding nothing back. Then we put the letter aside. Unlike journaling, we make a point of returning to the letter after some time has passed, whether it is a few hours, days, weeks, or months, depending on what feels appropriate to us, and we reread it. At that time we may want to write another letter that more accurately reflects our feelings in that moment. This can be repeated as often as needed to clarify feelings. Like journaling, writing letters we don't send helps ground our emotions on paper, which frequently helps us gain a different perspective.

I have had success using this method with my clients over the years, as in the case of Mary, who consulted me for depression after her mother died of cancer. Mary's grief was complicated by her ambivalence toward her relationship with her mother. Having had a deprived childhood, her mother tried to give Mary everything she had wanted for herself. She enrolled Mary in dance and music lessons at an early age, insisting that Mary perform in recitals and competitions. She expected Mary to achieve scholastically and socially in school, and she involved herself in every aspect of Mary's life. She showered Mary with praise when Mary met her expectations, and was highly critical when Mary fell short. Mary found herself emotionally dependent on her mother but at the same time angry and resentful for not being truly accepted. Mary never addressed these issues with her mother, who continued to be demanding until the end.

As part of our therapeutic work, Mary began writing letters to her mother. Her first letters were filled with anger and resentment. Expressing those feelings freely helped Mary access other underlying feelings, which she recorded in subsequent letters, such as the tremendous amount of hurt she experienced for not being accepted for herself and the negative impact this had on her self-acceptance. As Mary's feelings were expressed and processed, the blocked energy of the repressed emotions began to resolve and her depression lifted.

Mary's final letter was one from her mother to herself, written at my suggestion when I could see that she was near the completion of her therapeutic work. In it Mary demonstrated an amazing empathy for the pain behind her mother's attempts to right the wrongs of her own life through Mary, and she portrayed her mother's behavior as motivated by a loving, though misguided, desire for Mary's life to be better than her own. From this process of writing, Mary learned to separate her self-esteem from the perfectionist expectations of her mother, and she came to accept herself better. This expanded perspective helped Mary forgive her mother and complete her own healing.

SUMMARY

Impatience and irritability are common symptoms of stress. In their extreme forms they manifest as anger and rage. Given the high level of stress in contemporary life, it is no accident that murder and mayhem dominate the news. The documentary *Bowling for Columbine* revealed the alarming figure of over 11,000 shooting deaths in the United States each year. Compared to well below 200 deaths in other industrialized nations such as Great Britain and Canada, this is an alarming figure. Something is drastically wrong, and it clearly relates to our growing difficulties with managing our emotions under our present level of societal stress.

Skillful and constructive management of emotions is not only a critical aspect of transcending stress but also an essential element for the survival of a civilized society. It is crucial that we learn these skills and reduce the level of stress in our lives. It is equally crucial to teach our children these skills and avoid perpetuating a high level of stress. Managing our emotions wisely saves us from unnecessary self-generated stress and suffering on a personal level, and helps create a safer, gentler, and more compassionate world. ❧

We can learn to become more aware of what we are

thinking, and this awareness makes it possible to

disengage from negative thinking patterns.

CHAPTER 5

THINK BETTER AND FEEL BETTER

*T*he last chapter focused on understanding feelings and emotions and developing skills for managing them constructively. Because feelings are intricately connected to the thinking process, this chapter bridges these two domains and explores the dynamic relationship between cognition and emotions. We will distinguish between rational thinking and stimuli-driven thinking; discuss the power of the imagination and examine the impact of negative thinking; identify some common negative thinking patterns that exacerbate stress; and look to positive imagery and meditation as tools for calming our emotions and quieting our mind. Even though we cannot eliminate stressful events from our lives, we can effectively reduce much of the self-induced stress that is caused by an unexamined and untrained mind.

THE MULTI-FACETED MIND

The mind is an amazing organ. Like the operating system in a computer, it directs all our physiological, emotional, and mental processes. A primary function of the mind is to think. Yet, as we will see, not all thinking is constructive. Our ability to engage in rational thinking is a great gift, one that distinguishes us from the other members of the animal kingdom. Inductive reasoning enables us to formulate principles and theories; deductive reasoning enables us to draw conclusions. These mental functions make it possible for us to extrapolate data, identify patterns, consider consequences, draw conclusions, and make conscious choices. Without these processes, we could not have achieved the scientific progress and technological advances of today.

The mind also governs our stimulus-response function, which includes muscular reflexes, physiological processes such as the stress response, as well as stimuli-driven thinking. This type of thinking is qualitatively different from the rational thought processes mentioned above. It is governed by a different part of the mind and actually constitutes the majority of our thoughts. Our senses are stimulated by an event, and the stimulation triggers a train of thoughts. Instead of being purposeful and conscious, stimuli-driven thinking is automatic and tends to have more to do with our own concerns than with actual reality. For example, have you ever believed you were personally targeted by a remark, perhaps even constructed in your mind elaborate reasons as to why you were targeted, only to find out later that the remark had nothing to do with you? Unlike rational thinking processes, stimuli-driven thinking is generally not constructive.

STIMULI-DRIVEN THINKING AND STRESS

That the majority of our thinking belongs in the stimuli-driven category has tremendous implications when it comes to reducing stress. Since our vulnerability to stress depends on how we perceive the stress-inducing situation, how we think or how seriously we take our thinking is critical. From my decades of counseling, I have found that most of us do not question our thoughts until we are called to do so, usually by some event that has left us shaken. When we do begin to look deeper into our thinking, we are likely to find that there is a theme to our stimuli-driven thoughts. For example, we might find over time that underneath our thoughts lie certain beliefs, such as that people tend to think poorly of us, or that others cannot be relied upon, or that good things seldom happen to us. Stimuli-driven thoughts are rarely in our favor, and in fact, these thoughts relate more to our past conditioning and our self-concept than to the reality of the triggering events.

Let us take a look at how early stressful experiences can make us more prone to stimuli-driven thought patterns. The emotional energy of a very young child flows freely and comes to a natural resolution. His mental functions are not sufficiently developed for him to attribute intentionality or imagine causation. As the mind develops, however, its growing language skills and conceptual abilities not only enhance the maturing rational processes, but also embellish emotional experiences.

When growing children experience stressful events, they attribute reasons for them. Owing to their inexperience with life and to the naturally self-focused tendency of the young, these reasons are not always correct. For example, a parent's preoccupation or fatigue might be interpreted by the child as his not deserving love and attention; a parent's irritability might be seen by the child as her being somehow at fault. With their developing but not fully mature mental functioning, children need adults to help them modulate their feelings and guide them in their reasoning process. Without this mentoring, they are left believing that their stimuli-driven thoughts accurately reflect reality.

When stress is chronic, stimuli-driven thoughts form patterns that become automatically triggered by similar circumstances. These thought patterns haunt us until they are challenged and addressed. One common stimuli-driven thought pattern, as mentioned above, is the tendency to assume that we have done something wrong when we sense that someone is displeased, disappointed, or angry. Our mind becomes agitated as it tries to figure out what we did wrong, and we accordingly feel guilty, inadequate, frightened, or unjustly treated. These emotions generate more thinking, which in turn creates even more negative emotions, and we find ourselves trapped in a vicious cycle.

THE POWER OF IMAGINATION

As we can see from the above discussion, regardless of whether we interpret events accurately, the thinking-feeling cycle can powerfully affect us. This is because, in some cases, the mind does not distinguish between imagination and reality. The same physiological responses take place in either case. If we imagine we are eating a lemon, we salivate as though we can actually taste its sourness. If we imagine a prowler at the window, our muscles tighten and our breathing becomes shallow. If we anticipate failure, we experience all the accompanying feelings of shame and inadequacy; imagining abandonment will evoke separation anxiety. In other words, our mind can outsmart itself by generating imaginary scenarios and mistaking them for reality. Associated physiological responses are accordingly set off, which makes us feel worse and can also become harmful to our health.

Our imagination is so powerful that the use of positive imagery has become a healing practice in and of itself. Conversely, and just as significant for our purposes, negative imagery is equally powerful in terms of its adverse effects on us. Worrying is a form of imagery and a product of our imagination. It triggers the same stressful emotions and physiological responses as if what we worry about is actually happening. People who habitually think catastrophic thoughts regularly discharge stress hormones into their bloodstreams, the negative effects of which we have already examined. Similarly, negative beliefs about ourselves affect our physiology as though those beliefs were true. Anytime we engage in negative thinking or self-talk, we infuse ourselves with the energy of the accompanying negative emotions and suffer the corresponding physiological consequences.

Dr. Emoto, a Japanese scientist, conducted an interesting experiment that supports this idea. Dr. Emoto has discovered that words can have a profound effect on the formation of water crystals. By taping different words on glasses of water and then filming the water crystals through high-technology lenses, he discovered that water taped with words such as "love," "compassion," and "peace" generated beautiful crystal formations, whereas words such as "hate," "anger," and "shame" generated ugly, malformed crystals. If we were to consider that our body is composed of over 90 percent water, Dr. Emoto's work confirms even more urgently the need for us to be mindful of our thought processes.

SAMPLER OF HARMFUL THINKING PATTERNS

The Alarmist
The alarmist imagines a negative outcome for most situations and immobilizes himself from taking any constructive action. His thoughts frequently begin with the words, "What if." The alarmist thinks in terms of possibilities of what could happen, not in terms of probabilities or what is likely to happen. Since anything is always possible, the alarmist has unlimited and endless topics to worry about. As long as there is the most remote possibility of an undesirable result, he worries about that unlikely possibility and discharges stress hormones into his system. It is not difficult to see how habitually thinking this way promotes further anxiety, worry, and indecisiveness. While all of us might think like this occasionally, this tends to be an entrenched thought pattern for people with high levels of anxiety. It is not unusual to find this thinking pattern

in people suffering from chronic conditions such as fibromyalgia and chronic fatigue syndrome.

Joanne, a lovely young woman, came for psychotherapy when she was about six months into a relationship with Tim. She experienced mounting anxiety anytime Tim was more than fifteen minutes late for their planned activities. Her fear of abandonment precipitated anxiety-laden thinking, such as, "What if Tim has been hurt, or was killed, or has stopped loving me, or has met someone more interesting?" All of these negative images exacerbated her anxiety. This was a familiar pattern for Joanne, who had experienced similar problems in prior relationships. She could see that her need for constant reassurance was beginning to create difficulties between her and Tim.

Don suffered from hypertension and was referred by his physician to learn to manage stress better. Even though his business was very successful, Don worried constantly: What if something goes wrong with his suppliers? What if the location of his store becomes less desirable? What if his customers fall off and he can no longer meet his rent? While these are certainly important considerations for any business owner, Don worried about these possibilities almost continuously, without any indications that they would come to pass.

The Lamenter

Another negative thinking pattern manifests as a train of thoughts starting with the words "If only." *If only* I hadn't accepted that promotion, *if only* I had been nicer, *if only* we hadn't sold the house. This type of thinking consumes a great deal of emotional energy but serves no practical purpose. It differs qualitatively from the rational thinking process of trying to understand what happened in order to learn from the experience. The lamenter experiences regret whenever something goes awry, but this second-guessing only serves to undermine his self-confidence and destroy his peace of mind.

When we engage in regret, we forget that what might have happened, had we chosen the alternative, is a figment of our imagination and not reality. None of us could possibly know how things would be today had we accepted the other job offer, married the other person, relocated to another city, or chosen a different field of study. Nor can we predict how what we regret today will turn out in the future. At the time of my divorce, I was certain it was the worst thing that could ever happen to me. In retrospect, I know that event challenged all my preconceived ideas about how life was supposed to be, and that it became the impetus behind my interest in and dedication to growth and development over these last few decades.

This is not to say that there are no legitimate regrets. Our regrets are reality-based when we know that we have truly caused someone else harm. Such regrets, however, are not mental habits that kick into gear when we feel disappointed or unpleasantly surprised. Instead, true regret is a soft sadness deep inside, without words. We feel sad because we understand that there is nothing we can do to reverse what has happened, but this sadness is far gentler than guilt because we accept and forgive our frailty as imperfect beings. The constructive way of dealing with regret is to allow the feeling to pass through, to consider an apology if the apology will not cause the other person more harm, and to resolve to live our lives in a manner that will not create more regret for us in the future.

The Glass is Always Half-Empty
Sometimes negative thought patterns are triggered by good feelings rather than unpleasant ones, as though the person is unable to

tolerate feeling good. As a result, their focus keeps returning to what is not going right. Debbie, for example, who came to yoga almost immobilized with pain, began feeling significantly better after about a year of careful work. Whenever her improvement is acknowledged, however, she shifts the topic to the multitude of aches and pains she still experiences. If we call her attention to a posture she could not do before but which she can now do with ease, she invariably names the many other postures she still cannot do.

Another example is Jeannette, who cannot accept a compliment or be congratulated without launching into a long story about how messed up her life actually is. It is as though being messed up, inadequate, unable, or endowed with the worst luck has become an identity for these two women, both of whom suffer from depression. Sadly, regardless of how much better they might feel physically, they are not likely to feel better emotionally until they become aware of how their thought patterns truncate any possibility of experiencing joy, hopefulness, satisfaction, gratitude, and contentment.

BREAKING NEGATIVE THINKING PATTERNS

Even when these thought patterns are long-standing, they can still be successfully changed through awareness, intention, focused concentration, new skills, and persistence. Joanne, for example, took a multi-pronged approach. She learned and utilized breathing exercises to calm her down when she experienced mounting anxiety. She enrolled in a yoga class that shifted her energy out of her head and into her feet so she could become grounded in reality rather than dwell in her fearful imagination. Our therapy sessions focused on helping her become more familiar with her stimuli-driven thoughts so she could intervene, develop a more nurturing internal dialogue to enhance her ability to soothe herself, and habitually reality check so she can distinguish between possibility and probability.

The following are effective tools you can use for changing negative thought patterns.

Selective Focus

When I ask my clients whether they give more water and fertilizer to the flowers they plant in their garden or to the weeds that sprout uninvited, their answer is invariably the flowers. The same principle applies when it comes to our thinking. We do not want to water and fertilize thought patterns that cause us distress. Yet many of us do not realize that we can control where to focus our mind. This leaves us in a position in which we are not the masters of our mind. Instead, our mind masters us. When something troublesome happens, we are likely to succumb to a vicious cycle wherein the unpleasant emotions evoked by the event precipitate troublesome thoughts, which in turn evoke even more unpleasant feelings. This process subjects us to far more emotional turmoil than is usually warranted by the precipitating event.

We can learn to become more aware of what we are thinking, and this awareness offers us the freedom to disengage from negative thinking patterns. As we will see when we learn to meditate, observing our thought patterns is a different experience from being immersed in them. Consistently and persistently using conscious breathing to break the thought patterns that cause us distress will in time help us put these patterns to rest. Taking the example of Joanne again, her recovery was assured when she started to focus her attention on the reassuring facts of her life instead of the frightening scenarios concocted by her imagination.

An opportunity for selectively focusing my attention presented itself during a yoga retreat I co-led. A whirling ceiling fan came crashing down during our first evening program. Fortunately, the two students it hit were not seriously injured, but all of us felt so trau-matized that a pall descended over us. The joy and laughter of only a moment before dissipated into thin air. Throughout that night I had to actively dodge blaming thoughts and "what if" thinking, two lifelong habits I have worked hard to relinquish but which were evoked by the traumatic event. Instead, I focused on my breathing, on the necessity and practicalities of moving into another space, on the best way to facilitate healing for the group, and on how best to negotiate with the retreat facility so our needs could be met. This was not an easy process, and I had to repeatedly guide my thoughts back to constructive solutions.

Being able to maintain a positive attitude helped me conduct a congenial negotiation with the retreat center staff the following day. They gave us a different space to use and helped us move, which in turn helped to facilitate a resolution of the trauma for our group. We all ended up thoroughly enjoying the weekend in spite of the mishap, and felt good about our ability to deal with the unexpected in a positive manner. The way that weekend evolved is really a microcosm of the life process itself, which is filled with unexpected surprises, good and bad, that require our skillful management to avoid unnecessary suffering.

It is important we do not confuse selectively focusing our atten-tion with repressing our feelings. Feelings are experienced as a clear sensation or rush of energy. We have names for feelings, such as hurt, anger, sadness, joy, ecstasy, fear. I felt terrified that the ceiling fan could have seriously injured our students, frightened that it had ruined the retreat experience for them, and frustrated with the unfortunate turn of events. These feelings needed their full energetic expression because that was the only way they could be resolved. What selectively focusing our attention helps us avoid is not our feelings, but the mental embellishments to our emotions that may not be valid, such as attributing bad intentions to people who inadvertently hurt us, or painting pictures of ourselves as perennial victims. I did, for example, have transient thoughts that the universe was against me for allowing such a freak accident to occur, but I was able to remain disengaged from them because I recognized the pattern and knew from experience that allowing these thoughts to take root would have made me feel a lot worse.

Positive Imagery

While negative imagery can cause us more harm than we realize, the good news is that the corollary is also true. Positive imagery also has a powerful effect on us. If we imagine a pleasant experience, such as walking leisurely along the riverbank on a bright spring day, we will most likely find ourselves more relaxed and carefree. The efficacy of imagery has been confirmed by research for a wide range of purposes, from relieving anxiety and stress to the manifesting of our desires, even to the healing of chronic medical conditions such as cancer and heart disease. In fact, the use of healing imagery has become a therapeutic practice in and of itself, and you can easily learn to adapt it for yourself.

The key to effective imagery is to activate as many of the five senses as possible. To take the imagery of walking along a riverbank above, see what is around you, whether it is colors in the landscape, ripples in the flowing water, or white clouds against the blue sky; hear the river flowing, the flutter of butterfly wings, or the leaves rustling in the wind; smell the fragrance of the plants or the scent of spring in the air; and feel the sun and the breeze touching your skin, or your muscles moving as you walk along.

You can use imagery to influence how you feel by recalling those images that would elicit the feelings you want. For example, when Esther felt lonely during her trip back to college after spending a lovely Thanksgiving with her family, she recalled the loving faces of her family and the warmth of their love for each other. To enhance relaxation, I frequently employ the imagery of nature and the qualities of warmth and softness in the guided imagery I lead, ranging from soaking in a warm bath to lying on the beach with the sound of ocean waves in the background, or floating on a soft, cuddly cloud.

Imagery can also alleviate anticipatory anxiety and help prepare you for an event. When Don felt anxious at the prospect of giving a talk to a large audience, he recalled the last talk he gave and focused on the positive reception from his audience. If you have no such memory to draw on, you can borrow one. For example, to prepare for her first talk, Melinda recalled someone whose talk she had attended and enjoyed, and imagined herself similarly presenting with warmth and self-assurance. Many athletes also use imagery to prepare themselves, reviewing movements and imagining themselves at peak performance.

Research has found that imagery can also positively affect medical conditions. Instead of worrying about a health problem, for example, imagine yourself radiantly healthy and well. Or when recovering from surgery, imagine that you are surrounded by and infused with healing energy that will speed up your recovery. You can also imagine sending healing energy and love to others when you are concerned about their health.

In the example of Joanne, one of the positive imageries she used was to visualize herself confident and self-assured in a variety of situations, real or imagined. She practiced it when she woke up in the morning and before she fell asleep at night. Another was to visualize Tim behaving lovingly toward her as a replacement for the image of him abandoning her, which arose when her anxiety was triggered. She also regularly practiced the longer visualization for relaxation included at the end of this chapter.

Affirmations

Affirmations are positive statements we make to ourselves that can serve as excellent substitutes for negative thinking and self-talk. They provide us with imagery that will keep our emotions either neutral or positive. Affirmations are short, direct statements in the present tense, not intentions for the future: for example, "I am compassionate and kind" rather than "I will become compassionate and kind." Affirmations should not be stated in the negative. "I have radiant health" is more effective than "I will not be sick." These are two essential components for framing an effective affirmation.

We can use affirmations to replace negative thought patterns that exacerbate stress. For example, instead of "I'll never live this down," a negative statement that undermines our emotional resilience, we can tell ourselves, "I am the judge of my own behavior." In the example of Joanne, some of the affirmations she used to alleviate her anxiety included: "I am capable of making myself happy," "I trust that things happen as they are meant to," and "I can withstand adversity."

Meditation

Meditation is an ancient practice that trains us to detach from and rise above the agitations of our mind so we can be more present to our experiences. The mind is never idle. It is constantly producing thoughts. Contrary to popular misconceptions, meditation does not attempt to stop the mind from thinking or empty it. To do so would be impossible, since the function of the mind is to think. What we try to accomplish in meditation is to train ourselves to avoid getting lost in the transient, unproductive, idle chatter of our minds.

In meditation we develop the ability to detach from our thoughts and relate to them as impartial observers. Just as the ability to watch and monitor our feelings puts us in the driver's seat in relationship to our emotions, the ability to observe and monitor our thinking similarly puts us in charge. Being the observer in both situations helps us to avoid identifying with our experiences. We can think of meditation as a process for developing our internal observer to oversee the workings of our mind so we can have more clarity about ourselves and the world around us. Meditation relieves stress, improves concentration, and increases our sense of equanimity.

While there are a variety of ways to meditate, all of them choose a point of focus for the mind. This can be a mantra or sacred saying, our breath, bodily sensations, an image, or words that have personal meaning for us. What is most important but difficult to remember in practicing meditation is to avoid the trap of trying to do it right or constantly measuring our progress according to how still our mind increasingly becomes. Trying to achieve in meditation is contrary to its purpose, and the strain of trying too hard only triggers the stress response, thereby becoming counterproductive. Instead, practice tolerance when your mind wanders off the focus. When you find yourself lost in your thoughts, all that is necessary is for you to gently bring your attention back to your chosen point of focus. The goal is to know clearly what is happening in the present moment, including the fact that your mind has wandered again.

The following exercise is a simple way to meditate, that of being mindful. It is followed by a discussion of incorporating meditation into our daily lives in a practical way to alleviate stress.

EXERCISE 5—A Simple Meditation
Find a quiet place and set aside ample time. Whether you sit in a chair or cross-legged on the floor is not important. The outer form of sitting is not the essence of meditation. What is important is that you are comfortable and feel adequately supported to allow your spine to be upright and your chest to be open so your breath can flow easily. If you decide to sit in a chair, make sure your feet rest comfortably and completely on the floor. If you are short, use a footstool or a telephone book under your feet. If you are tall, pad your chair with a blanket so the height is right for your body.

Yoga was originally conceived to prepare the body for meditation. Many people find it easier to meditate after their yoga practice, since that is when their minds are more quiet, their breath more free, and their hips more open to allow their spine to be erect.

1.   Sitting quietly, turn your attention to your breathing. Notice the inhalations and exhalations. Do not strain and do not try to control your breathing.

2.   Notice the coolness of the breath entering your nostrils and notice your breath inside the body, where is goes, the route it travels. Notice the breath leaving your nostrils, warmer than when it entered.

3.   Let your breath and the way it moves through your body be the foreground of your attention, and let everything else recede into the background of your consciousness.

4.   If your mind wanders, as it is prone to do, gently bring it

back to your breath, the same way you would bring a puppy you are housebreaking back to the newspaper each time it wanders away.

5.   If you find your concentration wandering a lot, you can note your breath by saying "in" quietly to yourself as you inhale, and "out" as you exhale.

6.   Something else you can do when you find yourself distracted by thoughts is to pay attention not to the content of the thoughts but to the spaces between the thoughts.

7.   Without mental embellishments, periodically become aware of yourself sitting there, breathing and observing your breath.

Many teachers recommend meditating twenty minutes twice a day. If you can, doing so would be optimal. As for all practices, it is important to designate a specific time and place for medi-tation. My experience over the years, however, has been that most people find this schedule impossible. Because consistency and regularity is the most important, I suggest starting with just five to ten minutes if that is all the time you have, once a day if that is all you can manage, and augment this by interspersing shorter sessions throughout the day, even if it is just for a few breaths. I have found this abbreviated schedule more practical and sustainable for people under stress.

EXERCISE 6—Mindfulness in Our Daily Life
Once we familiarize ourselves with the art of meditation, we can incorporate the practice of mindfulness into daily activities. For the purpose of reducing stress, this technique is the most doable since it does not require setting aside special time, something already in short supply. After all, the whole purpose for meditating is to train the mind to focus on what we are doing rather than to wander off and think unproductive

thoughts. What better way to accomplish this than to utilize the very activities we already do as the venue for our meditation, and becoming more present to our experiences while engaged in them?

Thich Nhat Hanh, the well-known Vietnamese monk and master meditation teacher, popularized walking as a form of meditation. Many other activities, such as eating, washing the dishes, jogging, and pulling weeds are equally suitable for meditation. Begin by choosing one of these tasks and designating it as your meditation time. Then approach the task with reverence and do it slowly and mindfully. When you wash dishes, for example, only wash dishes. Avoid distractions such as planning the next day's list of things to do or having a negative dialogue in your mind about how much you dislike housework. You might notice the smell of the dish soap, the temperature of the water, the feel of the slippery soap suds, the sunshine streaming in through the window, the weight of the dishes in your hands. Similarly, if you decide to meditate while pulling weeds, focus only on pulling weeds. Do not have an imaginary argument with your gardener or spouse about the brown spot on the lawn or worry about how much you can get done. You might focus on the smell of the earth, the color of the plants, the sensation of tugging on the weeds till they finally pop out of the earth, the feel of the sun on your skin.

EXERCISE 7—On the Beach Imagery
We have said that imagery can be used for a variety of purposes. This is one of my favorite exercises for inducing a sense of ease and relaxation. It places you on the beach, but you can create your own imagery, substituting any other scenario you prefer. Just remember to involve all five of your senses as you allow

your imagination to serve you positively.

1.   Lie comfortably on your back. Be as comfortable as possible in the ways we have discussed previously, using an eye pillow if that is your preference or a support under your knees. Tune in to your breathing and allow all distractions to fade into the background.

2.   Imagine you are walking along a white sand beach. Feel the movement of your body, your hips, your legs, your arms. Feel the soft sand under your feet, the way it shifts as you walk. Feel the gentle warmth of the sun on your skin, tempered by a soft, soothing breeze.

3.   See the blue sky and the soft white clouds drifting by—their shapes and textures—and the deep green ocean waves, breaking into salty white foam as they reach the shore. Observe the shapes and colors around you.

4.   Hear the sound of the ocean waves as they crash against the shore. Hear the sound of seagulls, and perhaps children playing in the far distance. Listen to the silence between the different sounds.

5.   Smell the salt of the ocean, the smoke from a barbecue in the distance, or just the sweetness of your skin.

6.   As you walk, you come to a sheltered place that feels just right. You spread your beach towel on the sand. Feel yourself lying down on the towel and your body sinking softly into the sand.

7.   Feel the warmth of the sand seeping through your towel, the touch of the breeze on your skin and through your hair. Allow a wonderful sense of well-being to spread through you as you notice your breathing relax, your muscles relax, your bones relax, your inner organs relax.

8.   In this state of relaxation, you know with absolute certainty that all is well and as it should be. Let yourself be content and

satisfied with things just as they are in this precious moment.

9. You can rest in this state of well-being for as long as you like. Know that anytime you would like to return to this place, you have only to close your eyes, relax your breath, and allow these images to arise.

10. When you are ready to come out of your relaxation, give yourself plenty of time for the transition. Bend your knees and gently roll over to one side when you are ready. Softly open and close your eyes a few times, re-engaging with your environment slowly, then gently use your hands to push yourself into a sitting position, relishing your journey to the beach.

SUMMARY

Automatic stimuli-driven thinking, triggered when our senses become stimulated, is different from rational and purposeful cognitive processes. The negative images created by such thinking generate in us the same feelings and physiological processes had these imagined scenarios been real. A dynamic relationship exists between stimuli-driven thinking and our emotions, forming a self-reinforcing loop and generating stress that in time becomes harmful to our health.

Selectively focusing our attention through positive imagery, affirmations, and meditation is an excellent way for changing negative thought patterns. Through these practices we can replace negative images, change our internal dialogue, disrupt the vicious cycle of negative thinking and painful emotions, and improve our health. Like all the exercises we have introduced, these techniques require practice and familiarity before they can be truly helpful. Try them and find for yourself the ones that are particularly suitable for you. ❧

Letting go of fear frees our creativity

and enhances our gusto for life.

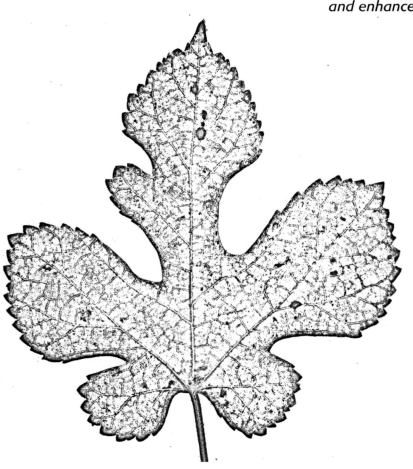

CHAPTER 6

A NEW LOOK AT OLD FEARS

*T*he last few chapters addressed feelings, emotions, and thoughts as we experience them in the present, and offered strategies for managing them judiciously. In this chapter we move from the realm of the conscious to that of the subconscious, to examine fear-based patterns that are no longer in our awareness but which nevertheless can, when triggered, become primary motivators for our actions and decisions. It is easy to mistakenly think of these often subtle and familiar patterns as part of our personality and not realize how much they distort our perception, interfere with our ability to respond freely to current circumstances, and perpetuate a state of chronic stress that compromises our physical and mental well-being. It is only when we free ourselves from these deeply ingrained fears that we realize how much we have been inhibited from coming fully into the freedom and joy that is our birthright.

Drawing from contemporary psychology and from theories of energy, we will explore fear-based patterns as blocked energy resulting from trauma. To sharpen our recognition of fear-based patterns, we will view examples of ways in which deep-seated fears might manifest in ordinary lives and how fear, on a collective level, has permeated our society. Avenues for healing will be presented, including self-inquiry, an essential yogic process for enhancing awareness to identify and dissolve fear-based tendencies, as well as mindfulness meditation, psychotherapy, and energy unblocking methods that are now available.

TRAUMA

In its definition of trauma, the *Diagnostic and Statistical Manual of Mental Disorders* requires the triggering event to meet the objective criteria of being unusual and outside of normal human experience. Similarly, we tend not to think of ourselves as having been traumatized unless the triggering event was of the magnitude of war, rape, or natural disaster. In my experience of working with energy-based trauma release methods, however, I have found that people are traumatized far more frequently than this formal definition or our expectations recognize. We can become traumatized by experiences within our ordinary lives, such as feeling betrayed by a friend or loved one, feeling humiliated in a social situation, being blamed for something we did not do, suffering a car accident, or being screamed at in anger.

For our purposes, trauma refers to our intense reaction when we feel overwhelmed by a disturbing event. The traumatic reaction, therefore, is subjective, and depends on our unique vulnerabilities and past experiences. In other words, trauma occurs when we experience overwhelming and excessive stress, and traumatic experiences are individual and subjective.

TRAUMA AND BLOCKED ENERGY

After we experience a traumatic event, if we are able to satisfactorily resolve within our mind what has transpired, the experience will eventually lose its emotional intensity and take its place as a part of our memory. This resolution usually occurs when we gain an expanded perspective, whether by talking with supportive people who understand the experience, reading educational information, or going through some other process that facilitates healing. We may thereafter experience faint echoes of the original emotions when we recall the trauma, but not their original intensity.

Unfortunately, many traumatic experiences, especially those that occurred during our childhood, are not adequately resolved. We may have felt too ashamed, guilty, or afraid to confide in anyone; we may not have been in the habit of confiding in others; or perhaps the response we received was inappropriate or non-supportive. It is not unusual, after all, for a victim of trauma to be blamed, judged, and thus further traumatized.

When a traumatic experience is not fully resolved and viewed from an expanded perspective, the emotional energy generated from the experience cannot find resolution and becomes blocked. As a result, the experience cannot be satisfactorily integrated as part of the memory. In this way, over time, we can accumulate energy blockages that interfere with how we function. An example of an energy blockage we have all experienced is the replaying of an unpleasant interaction over and over in our mind, long after the actual event is over. Our energy seems centered on that one incident, leaving us unable to move forward. Stuck energy prevents people from speaking up assertively on their own behalf, even though they understand and agree that doing so would benefit them.

ENERGY BLOCKAGE AND FEARS

Energy blockages many times manifest as phobias or unreasonable fears, such as the fear of flying, heights, small spaces, riding in elevators, the sight of blood, or driving across bridges. These fears may be constantly present, or they may manifest only after subsequent experiences that retraumatize. After 9/11, for example, there was an increase in my psychotherapy practice of clients seeking treatment for fears of flying and driving over bridges, as well as unfounded fears of dying, losing loved ones through death, and traveling out of town. Less dramatically but more insidiously, blockages can also manifest as performance anxiety, excessive guilt, food cravings, food allergies, grudges, and prolonged bereavements.

More subtly and pervasively, blocked energy can simmer just below the surface and distort our perception, trapping us behind lenses of fear. We experience the world as an unsafe place. We anticipate phantom risks where none exist. Our actions, decisions, and relationships become defensive in nature, based on the avoidance of a greater evil rather than on what is appropriate or optimally beneficial. When animals are frightened, they tend to run away, freeze, or attack. Similarly, when we are rooted in fear, we might avoid a situation, hesitate to act, or react precipitously with anger, suspicion, or flight. All these responses based on imagined danger are likely to make our situations worse and create additional stress for us.

ILLUSTRATIONS OF DEEP-SEATED FEARS

As we have mentioned, deep-seated fears manifest in our lives in such subtle and insidious ways that we can easily miss their presence and become accustomed to functioning within the limitations they impose. The following vignettes are drawn from my psychotherapy practice. They are about intelligent, ordinary people whose difficulties, in the larger scheme of things, were not great. Nevertheless, unconscious fears left from traumatic experiences hindered them from living to the fullest and added unnecessary stress to their lives. Read them with an ear tuned for notes of familiarity, whether in relationship to your own tendencies or to those of others.

Susan, whose husband confessed to having had a brief affair on a business trip, was unable to heal and move forward in her marriage and life. She had been deeply affected by betrayals of trust in her parents' marriage from an early age, and her husband's infidelity triggered one of her deepest fears. Even though her husband expressed sincere remorse and a renewed sense of commitment to their marriage, she continued to be plagued by fears of betrayal. She questioned him incessantly about the reasons for his infidelity, his present feelings toward herself and the other woman, and the details of his activities during the workday. Her fear-based behaviors not only kept the trauma alive and prevented her from healing, but in time also became an independent source of stress for the marriage.

Stephen, having been orphaned at an early age, lived life cautiously and was fearful of change. He had worked for the same firm all his adult life. Following a change of management, Stephen found his workplace increasingly oppressive and intolerable. He had enough years of employment to retire, and in fact, had received an attractive offer for part-time employment from a different firm. Even though the combined income from his early retirement and his new employment would exceed his full-time earnings, his fear of change immobilized him from taking constructive action. Stephen sought therapy when his symptoms of stress began to overwhelm him.

Emily, who grew up in a chaotic and unpredictable environment, shielded herself from her fears by attempting to keep her life under rigid control. When anything pertaining to her or her family threatened to move outside her sphere of influence, Emily responded by trying to exert even greater control. This was an unconscious defensive maneuver. Indeed, she experienced her point of view as being better, right, or more practical, and she usually felt frustrated, hurt, and angry when her family and friends were reluctant to follow her lead. Her husband, a relatively passive and easygoing man, went along with Emily's management of their finances, their lifestyle, their friendships, the parenting of their three children, even the clothes they wore. Life proceeded in relative peace until the children reached adolescence and their need for more autonomy came into direct conflict with Emily's need for control. Family conflicts escalated to such a degree that they sought professional help.

To escape from her fears of being alone and unloved, Liz kept herself constantly busy. She made friends with people with whom she had little in common and engaged in activities in which she had no real interest. She had difficulty saying no to unreasonable requests and asserting her boundaries when she felt intruded upon. While her many friendships completely occupied her time, Liz did not experience the satisfaction of feeling fully understood or cared about. She continued to experience a deep sense of loneliness in her life, which brought her to therapy.

Sally, a beautiful and bright woman, grew up poor. Her primary goal in life was to make certain she would never again experience the social humiliations she had suffered in school. She did well scholastically and worked hard in sales after graduation. She married a wealthy, successful man who provided her with the lifestyle she sought but who was emotionally unavailable, exacting in his expectations, and highly controlling. Despite having achieved her goal of financial security and social status, Sally was not happy and suffered from periodic episodes of depression, for which she sought help.

Bob was raised by strict immigrant parents who were underemployed and had to pinch pennies to survive. He was taught never to spend money unnecessarily. Even though he earned an excellent salary and had discretionary money to enjoy, Bob continued to be extremely frugal. He resisted participating in gift giving for birthdays and holidays, ate only at restaurants for which he had coupons, stayed at the most basic hotels when traveling, and scrimped in a variety of other ways. When his wife began working outside the home, and this frugality was no longer based on any perceivable necessity, they began having serious conflicts over the differences in their spending preferences. Bob finally consented to come in for couples therapy when his wife threatened to leave.

My own deep-seated fears came from experiencing a war, a revolution, and an evacuation, during which my father was killed. Subsequently my family and I immigrated three times. All this happened before I turned fourteen. The trauma and stress from those experiences left its mark. I felt unsafe and easily threatened. I was fearful of betrayal, rejection, and being taken advantage of. Not only did these fears make collaboration with others extremely difficult for me, but I developed a defensive, tough exterior that kept me trapped in the very isolation I needed to alleviate. It was only by identifying and releasing the fears behind my façade that I was able to create a less stressful life.

COLLECTIVE FEAR

Deeply ingrained individual fears accumulate and affect the functioning of a whole society. *Bowling for Columbine*, the documentary mentioned in an earlier chapter, concluded that the higher incidence of death by shooting in the United States as compared to other developed countries is not because of unemployment, poverty, or easy access to guns. Very similar circumstances exist across the border in Canada, yet its annual number of deaths by shooting is well under 200, as compared to more than 11,000 in the United States. The filmmaker proposed that the higher level of violence in American society is the result of a higher level of collective fear.

The idea that a society might be driven by fear is not an unreasonable proposition. More and more buildings have bars on their windows and doors. Alarm systems in cars, businesses, and homes have become standard features, and it has become common practice to hire private security personnel to safeguard shopping centers and social functions. During my travels overseas, I have noticed that U.S. consulates tend to stand out from neighboring buildings, distinguished by heavy barricades.

Anger and rage, the emotional precursors of violent behavior, are usually secondary emotions that cover up the primary emotions of fear and terror. In other words, aggressive behaviors are, more often than not, the vehicles for unleashing fears we are unable to acknowledge or address in more constructive ways. If we were to consider the war in Iraq in this light, we might see it as the outward manifestation of a collective unresolved trauma, terror, and sense of helplessness following the national tragedy of 9/11. Unfortunately, aggression and violence only breed more fear and terror, setting in motion vicious, unending cycles.

Turning the tide of this rising level of fear and violence is a difficult process, and it is not likely that solutions will come from any political leadership. Each of us must take steps to release our individual fears and heal our rifts with other people. Instead of seeing each other through adversarial eyes and highlighting our differences, we can reconnect with our spiritual roots and remember that all of us come from the same source and are one with each other. Our well-being is inextricably intertwined with that of all others. Kindness, compassion, tolerance, and collaboration go a long way toward creating trust; divisiveness, aggression, antagonism, and opposition serve only to raise the level of our collective fear and mistrust. Each of us must choose whether we want to create communities of mutual support and nurturing or become increasingly isolated in our self-righteousness and intolerance.

REMEDIES

There are now energy-unblocking procedures that produce astonishing results. Many specific fears that used to take months and sometimes years of talk therapy or desensitization to resolve can now be dissolved instantly, once the stuck energy is unblocked. These fears include the phobias and anxieties listed earlier, as well as food cravings. It was through the use of these methods with my clients that I deepened my understanding of emotions as energy.

Methods for releasing stuck energy behind specific fears include: TFT, or Thought Field Therapy; EMDR, or Eye Movement Desensitization and Reprocessing; EFT, or Emotional Freedom Techniques; and Quantum Techniques. New systems are evolving all the time. These methods work on the emotional body the same way that acupuncture and acupressure work on the physical body, by unblocking stuck energy or chi. Non-specific difficulties, such as generalized anxiety and fear-based patterns, however, are not as effectively resolved as yet by these methods, and require awareness-based processes such as those discussed below.

SELF-INQUIRY

Holistic yoga recommends self-inquiry as an essential practice. When we impartially observe and delve into our emotions and the workings of our mind, we open ourselves to a deeper awareness of our inner processes. Self-inquiry is invaluable for uncovering the fears that might be interfering with our ability to live to our fullest potential. Excellent vehicles for self-study include Iyengar yoga, through which we increase our awareness and concentration by focusing on bodily sensations, physical alignment, and subtle muscular movements; mindfulness meditation, through which we increase our self-understanding by observing our breath, sensations, emotions, and thought patterns; and a more generally introspective orientation, through which we examine and re-examine the motivations behind our actions, decisions, and habitual responses.

To practice self-inquiry in the present context, return to the illustrations and notice whether any of the examples of fear-based living strike a familiar chord when you read them. If so, identify the nuances of your own fears that might be reflected and the subtle ways your fears might manifest to block your spontaneous functioning. Another way to begin self-study in the context of discovering deeply seated fears is to assess how you go about making decisions and consider whether that process has generally been easy or stressful for you. Do you, for example, tend to be so concerned about possible negative outcomes that it becomes difficult for you to act, or might you find the tension of not knowing so difficult to contain that you tend to act precipitously?

Pay careful attention to the decisions facing you now, and ask yourself whether the solutions you are considering take into account your best interests or whether they might be arising out of an avoidance of some imagined pitfall. Reach into your memory bank and notice whether there are familiar patterns of avoidance. If your sense of avoidance is strong, delve a little deeper and see whether you might be able to identify the underlying fears. Recall decisions you made but are not happy with. Review them in terms of whether they were based on fear. Use all the information you gather nonjudgmentally and deepen your understanding of your ingrained patterns. Self-inquiry is not an easy practice, and it requires persistence. Honest observations frequently reveal things that can be initially unpleasant for us to own. Avoid self-recrimination or blaming others, both of which waste energy and serve no positive purpose. Use the self-calming skills we have explored in earlier chapters, especially conscious breathing and journaling, to support yourself and allow the past to be your source of wisdom for the future. A friend engaged in a similar process, a support group, or a skilled psychotherapist can all provide excellent support for you on your journey of self-discovery.

EXERCISE 8—Expanding Meditation Skills
Following the format in Exercise 5, sit quietly and turn your attention to your breath. Over time, you can gradually expand your awareness to incorporate any of the following as focal points for your attention, noticing and observing but not getting involved or lost in them.

1. Bodily Sensations: Notice the sensations in your body. You might notice places that feel good and places that feel uncomfortable. Even though your attention might first be drawn to the uncomfortable sensations, over time you might realize that all sensations are part of your total experience. You might also notice that minor discomforts usually do not last if you choose

to sit still and allow them to be. In this way the experience of our meditation approximates life, encompassing the good and bad within the totality of experience as it continuously changes and transforms.

2. Your Environment: Notice the sounds around you. Notice that, if you stay neutral and avoid either wishing them away or wanting them to last, they quickly become part of the background of your experience, as your breath or bodily sensations remain in the foreground. You can also notice the temperature of your skin, where you and your environment meet. Again, try to notice and not get distracted by your preferences for the temperature. In this way you are training yourself in the art of detachment.

3. Your Thoughts: You can also consider your thoughts as objects for meditation. This, however, can be tricky, since you are asked to only notice the thoughts and not become involved with them. For example, you might note that you are planning, complaining, rehearsing, or explaining. Then just let the thoughts go. Over time you might discover a pattern to your thoughts, and this will significantly deepen your understanding of yourself.

SUMMARY

Most of us have experienced minor traumas in our life that have not been fully resolved. These are embedded in our psyche as fears around which we organize our perception and responses. Organizing ourselves around fear and avoidance is fundamentally different from functioning freely. Fear and avoidance evoke a state of hyper-vigilance and maintain a level of stress hormones in our body that interferes with our health, limits our vision of what is possible, and short-circuits our intuitive abilities.

In this chapter we turned from tending to our immediate experiences to the more introspective process of identifying and releasing embedded fears. We introduced the practice of self-inquiry and expanded meditation skills, both of which support the inward journey. While self-inquiry can be a difficult process, it is important to remember that it becomes immensely gratifying when we persist, rewarding us with the precious gifts of awareness, self-knowledge, and wisdom. In the long run, an intimate relationship with our multi-dimensional selves and an expanded understanding of the reality around us enables us to live our lives with greater fulfillment, satisfaction, and the least amount of stress. ❧

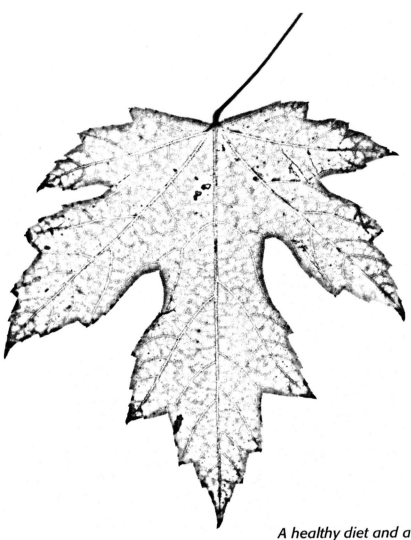

A healthy diet and a lifestyle that flows

in congruence with nature is the

cornerstone of physical well-being.

CHAPTER 7

THE ROAD TO HEALTH AND WELLNESS

*N*ow that we can calm our nervous system and quiet our mind, we can turn our attention to our physical well-being. The use of food, alcohol, drugs, and sensory stimulation as fast but ultimately harmful avenues for relieving stress is so prevalent in our society that changing poor dietary and lifestyle habits is seldom sustainable without first developing effective skills for relieving stress. People who use food as their primary form of stress relief, for example, find it near impossible to maintain healthy eating habits for any length of time, and those who habitually rush around are not likely to succeed in creating a lasting healthy daily routine.

A healthful diet and a lifestyle that flows in congruence with nature is the cornerstone of physical well-being. It is astonishing the degree to which adjustments in our diet and lifestyle can help correct a plethora of problems, including lethargy, chronic fatigue, insomnia, obesity, chronic pain, high cholesterol, hypertension, and more. Dr. Dean Ornish, based on his extensive research on heart disease and cancer, has found diet and lifestyle changes to be the treatment of choice for these conditions, and he uses them as the primary interventions in his world-famous treatment programs. Dr. Andrew Weil likewise emphasizes the important role played by diet and lifestyle when it comes to maintaining our health.

Ayurveda, the ancient energy-based science of health and longevity, similarly utilizes diet and lifestyle as its primary preventative interventions. This chapter presents some simple, health-enhancing principles and practices that can be integrated into our lives without undue complications.

Understanding ancient Ayurveda and contemporary Western medicine in terms of their fundamental differences as well as how they complement each other enables us to draw from both systems and increase our options for maintaining wellness. This chapter ends with two short yoga sequences that support muscular-skeletal health, improve energy and a sense of vitality, and increase physical flexibility. These sequences can be easily linked with the one at the end of Chapter 9 for a longer practice.

REVERENCE FOR THE BODY

While we can feel immensely grateful to live in an era in which laser surgery, joint replacements, organ transplants, and numerous other medical procedures can prolong life and lessen physical limitations, we must at the same time resist being lulled into a state of complacency about our body. We still need to do our part to actively care for our health. Despite our illusions of indestructibility, we are mortal beings, and we are more fragile than we would like to believe. The incredible self-regulating capacity of our physiological processes and muscular-skeletal structure can compensate for the neglect or misuse of our body for only so long without serious consequences. For example, our back does not suddenly give out one day because we sneezed or bent down to tie our shoes. The problem was a long time in the making, but we were not aware of all the compensatory maneuvers our spine and the muscles surrounding it were making before this final collapse. Surgical procedures do not really make us as good as new, and pharmaceuticals have the potential to cause serious side effects. The only way we can truly live a long and healthy life is by diligently caring for our body.

There is a difference between understanding something intellectually and really knowing it with our total being. Most of us take our body for granted until we have an emotional experience of our vulnerability, such as being faced with a health crisis or the loss of someone we love. Even then our minds can rationalize and overwhelm our innate wisdom. We find it easy to ignore symptoms or postpone treatment, and we are assisted in our negligence by the overabundance of over-the-counter remedies that mask symptoms but do not address underlying problems. A surprising number of people give themselves less routine care and attention than they do their pets or their automobile. However we rationalize this behavior, the reality is that we simply do not accord our health the priority it needs and deserves.

Neglecting one's physical well-being is not a natural tendency in the animal kingdom, where survival is the first order of the day. Animals instinctively refrain from eating what is not good for them, rest or hibernate when it is time, and withdraw in order to heal when they are injured. Because they do not have our cognitive capacity, animals are unhindered by ideas of how they should be or what others might think of them, and they do not rationalize themselves into self-destructive behavior patterns. Many of my psychotherapy clients, the majority of whom are intelligent professionals suffering from stress, realize during the therapy process that they have neglected their physical well-being because they have accorded more importance to being successful than to being healthy and well.

EAST MEETS WEST

Every system has its strengths and weaknesses. Sometimes a system's shortcomings are inherent in the very factors that give rise to its strengths. The following comparative discussion of Eastern and Western medical systems is not intended to present one as being superior or inferior to the other. That would not be true. My point is that the two systems are complementary to each other, that each has its own areas of expertise. This is a position that is becoming more and more recognized in the medical field. In fact, what used to be referred to as "alternative health care" is now often termed "complementary medicine."

Western medicine and its technology are exceptionally effective at diagnosing and treating acute physical problems. It is truly amazing how many body parts can be transplanted, replaced, or repaired today, and how much our life expectancy has increased from that of past generations. We have incredible knowledge of genetics; we can detect birth defects with high accuracy; and we might, controversially, even be on the verge of replicating life itself. Having had cataract surgery and experienced a dramatic improvement in my eyesight, I feel immensely grateful to live in an era in which failing eyesight is no longer an immutable factor of aging.

Western medicine's efficacy in treating acute problems derives from its focus on eradicating identified symptoms, and this capability is further enhanced by the trend toward specialization. Diagnosis and treatment are so efficient and precise it boggles the mind, and someone with intense pain can receive immediate relief. This very strength, however, has its drawbacks. The vague experiences of "dis-ease" that precede symptom manifestation and serve as warning signals are troublesome for

Western medicine to address because specific symptoms are absent. Also, as we have already mentioned, it is easy to confuse symptom relief with remedying an underlying problem. There is the danger that the treatment might be considered complete, even though the underlying problem remains unaddressed.

For example, cortisone shots are commonly given for muscular pain. This was the treatment for my chronic neck pain for several years before I discovered yoga, which not only taught me how to stretch and relieve the muscular tension in my neck, but also improved my posture so I no longer held my body in the position that led to the problem in the first place. Similarly, taking medication to reduce acidity is important for treating acid reflux, but avoiding certain foods and not eating within three hours of bedtime is equally important for correcting the underlying problem.

While the specialization of Western medicine makes for more in-depth expertise within each specialty, this strength brings with it the danger of reductionism. The focus is not on the whole person as a self-regulating system. It is not unheard of, for example, for a practitioner to miss the patient as a person and identify them with their illness, referring to them as "the gall bladder problem" or "the hip replacement." This attitude can have a subtly dehumanizing effect and hinder the patient's recovery. Also, the very treatment of symptoms in one part of the body may create problems in another. For instance, certain medications for high cholesterol can inhibit sexual arousal as well as compromise immune system functioning. It is alarming to learn that as many as 40 percent of illnesses today are iatrogenic, or induced by medical treatment.

A third difficulty in Western medicine results from another of its strengths: its reliance on objective research and data. Treatment is based on what is appropriate for the average person, or the majority of people. None of us, however, is exactly average.

In contrast, Ayurveda and other Eastern systems of medicine focus on the individual as a self-regulating energy system that follows distinct principles. Wellness is regarded as the byproduct of a system in good energetic balance, and symptoms are seen as indicators for how the system might be out of balance. Treatment focuses, therefore, not on eradicating symptoms but on restoring balance to the organism as a whole. This restoration is based on what the normal balance is for that individual, as might be determined through the person's pulse and a very detailed history of their present physiological functioning and living habits. Because it takes time to restore a system to balance, however, Ayurveda is unable to provide the immediate relief that can be delivered by the Western system.

The methodology of Ayurveda consists of a proper diet, a healthy lifestyle, herbal supplements, and cleanses. It would be inaccurate to say that the Western approach ignores lifestyle and diet, since there are numerous research studies on these topics. However, these studies are also symptom- or disease-focused. For example, one study found a correlation between drinking fruit juices or red wine and lower incidences of Alzheimer's disease in later life; another found a correlation between eating shellfish and a healthy libido; a third discovered a relationship between consuming fiber and reduced incidences of colon cancer. Without a coherent overall theory of wellness, it is difficult to intelligently incorporate these piecemeal findings into a meaningful dietary program.

To illustrate the differences between the two approaches, let us look at the situation of someone suffering from chronic heartburn and acne. Western medicine is likely to view these as separate conditions to be treated by a gastrointestinal specialist and a dermatologist respectively. The primary treatments are likely to be separate medications to neutralize the symptoms, such as antacids and ointments.

The Ayurvedic physician, on the other hand, is likely to see these as related problems, resulting from too much heat or fire energy in the body. Treatment is likely to include dietary and lifestyle changes supported by herbal supplements, and possibly timely cleanses designed to restore balance to the whole system. Dietary recommendations might include the elimination of heating foods such as peanuts, red meat, and foods that are highly spiced or deep fried. Special breathing practices and yoga postures that have a cooling effect might be suggested, and because fire energy relates to aggression, anger, and striving, these emotions might also be addressed.

To use the two systems in a complementary manner, we could consider the use of digestive enzymes or antacids for the heartburn, and ointments or special soaps for acne. These remedies address the symptoms and alleviate immediate discomfort. Concurrently, we could also make the recommended dietary and lifestyle changes, as well as addressing our emotions, to take care of the underlying issues.

WELLNESS

Wellness does not merely refer to the absence of symptoms. It also signifies the presence of subtle, subjective, and not readily quantifiable experiences that are the byproducts of a well-functioning, self-regulating system. My experiences of wellness over the years have included feelings of lightness in the body, steady energy throughout the day, a clear mind, a sense of vitality, a level mood, smooth digestion, and restful sleep. These were not permanent states. They fluctuated according to what I ate, how much I ate, when I ate, when I went to bed, and my activities during the day. If I wanted to experience these states in a more lasting manner, I had to actively keep dietary and lifestyle variables fairly constant.

As we can see, the language of wellness is less the language of Western medicine and more that of Ayurveda. One way of looking at this is that the more directly symptoms are related to an actual problem, the more effective Western medical treatment is likely to be. When it comes to appendicitis, stroke, pneumonia, heart attack, or a broken limb, for example, Western medicine is, without question, the treatment of choice. For the creation and maintenance of wellness, on the other hand, Ayurveda offers a comprehensive system of principles and practices from which we can draw.

Ayurveda's teachings resonate with common sense, and they can frequently be verified directly through our own experience when we pay attention to our body and consider the right variables. For example, many of the students from my wellness workshops, once they made the right associations, felt that their stomachs were more acidic after they ate deep-fried foods. Similarly, they found that eating late at night disturbed their sleep. So keep an open mind as you read what follows, give some of the suggestions a try, and notice for yourself whether they are helpful to you. It is important to make only one or two changes at a time, so you can more clearly monitor and identify their effects on you, and to avoid becoming overwhelmed. Our discussion of Ayurveda is limited to practical applications and not intended to be comprehensive, which would be far beyond the scope of this book. I have also intentionally avoided Sanskrit terms, to keep the reading simple. Readers who would like to learn more about this ancient holistic system of self-care can refer to the resources section for more in-depth reading.

ALIGNING WITH NATURE

We have said previously that each of us is a microcosm of the universe, formed of the same energies as all of nature and governed by the same laws. Therefore, a basic Ayurvedic guiding principle for optimum health is to, as much as possible, live congruently with nature. For example, rising when the sun rises and retiring when the sun sets is a practice that is congruent with the forces of nature. Staying up at night and sleeping through the day is not. Eating when we are hungry and abstaining when we are full is congruent with nature. Eating before we are hungry, denying ourselves food when we experience hunger, and stuffing ourselves beyond full is not natural. Eliminating bodily wastes as we experience the need follows the dictates of nature while holding back does not, and receiving our nutrients and vitamins through fresh and healthy foods is more congruent with nature than receiving them through supplements.

We can see evidence of this principle in action. While advances in medical science have conquered such devastating diseases as the plague, smallpox, and polio, new difficulties, such as stress-related diseases, have evolved as technology and the modern lifestyle distance us further and further from nature. We speak of jet lag when we defy gravity and speed across time zones;

and we experience similar symptoms of fatigue, sleep disturbances, and reduced vitality when we work rotating shifts, habitually stay up late, or in other ways ignore the cycles of day and
night. Incidences of chronic pain, obesity, digestive tract problems, immune system dysfunctions, allergies, and asthma have
increased dramatically as we lead sedentary lives in artificial
lighting; eat genetically engineered, chemical-sprayed, highly
processed foods at irregular hours; and pollute the air we
breathe and the water we drink with exhaust fumes and indus-
trial waste.

A correlation between the increase in Type 2, or adult onset,
diabetes and the consumption of artificially sweetened soft
drinks has recently been found. The pancreas, which discharges
insulin when the taste buds are stimulated by sugary tastes,
becomes confused when it responds to the taste of artificially
sweetened drinks but finds no actual sugar for the insulin to
process. Over time, the pancreas self-regulates and gradually
stops discharging insulin, treating all sugary tastes as false
alarms, even when there is real sugar to be processed. It would
seem that we simply cannot try to fool Mother Nature without
suffering the consequences.

WE ARE WHAT WE EAT
Another key Ayurvedic teaching is that the foods we eat and the
liquids we drink constitute the materials with which we renew
our body at the cellular level. This simple principle seems self-
evident and aligns with the principles of Western science. It is
not terribly puzzling that obesity and associated health problems are escalating in our society when we consider that the
average person is rebuilding himself with the fat and chemicals

from hamburgers, chips, hot dogs, soft drinks, steaks, French fries, intoxicants, and processed foods. For example, in the documentary *Super Size Me*, the filmmaker's health is seriously compromised after only one month of unhealthy eating. If we consider that our cellular regeneration takes place continuously, it would follow that such a decline could happen so rapidly.

Food not only affects our physical health but also dramatically influences our mental well-being. The rude, obnoxious, and antagonistic behavior of developmentally challenged students in a Wisconsin alternative high school changed dramatically for the better after the principal replaced vending machines with water coolers and changed the cafeteria's offerings from hamburgers and French fries to fresh vegetables, fruits, and whole-grain breads. Several research studies have shown a relationship between a higher IQ and the reduction of sugar and fat in one's daily diet. Studies have also shown a decrease in aggressive behavior in prison inmates who were given vitamin supplements. If we consider that our brain cells are also regenerated by what we eat, these findings make complete sense. Instead of building more expensive prisons, imagine our society spending its resources on healthier diets for crime prevention.

The two principles above work in tandem. As we choose healthier materials for the regeneration of our cells, for example, the principle of aligning with nature can serve as a helpful guide. Fresh, local, in-season produce is more aligned with nature than fruits and vegetables that have been harvested prematurely, stored, shipped long distances, genetically altered, or canned. The less processed the food, the closer it is to nature and, therefore, the better for us. An indication that food has been overly processed is when we can no longer recognize its natural ingredients, such as is often the case with cold cereals and "nutrition" bars.

Some contamination of our food is more difficult to detect. Our meat supply, for example, is a matter for serious concern. Most animals are raised unnaturally and under stressful conditions, such as crowded pens with artificial lighting, and they are fed hormones to accelerate their growth. Because animals, just like humans, discharge stress hormones into their bloodstream, it is difficult to imagine that their meat is not saturated with substances that will in turn affect us negatively when we consume their flesh. Our supply of fish and shellfish also comes into question when we consider the polluted state of many rivers and oceans.

For these reasons, Ayurveda considers purified water, organically grown and genetically unaltered produce, free-range poultry, and animals not fed artificial hormones to be the only acceptable food supply. Similarly, Ayurveda encourages us to eat freshly prepared vegetarian foods in the right combinations, rather than stale leftovers. Eating this way may cost more, but if we truly acknowledge that what we eat constitutes our building blocks from the cellular level up through all the dimensions of our being, we may find that this expenditure is more pertinent to our well-being than a newer car, bigger house, or costly vacation.

On an even more subtle level than ingesting chemicals, pesticides, and hormones, we absorb the energies of what we consume. Ayurveda recommends that meals be prepared with a loving heart so that the foods are imbued with positive energy. If the cook is angry and agitated, this energy is absorbed into the food and in turn absorbed by the diner. Imagine being fed food prepared by someone angrily banging pots and pans around, as opposed to having a meal that was lovingly prepared for you. It might be useful to remember this principle and consider the morale of the restaurant staff when selecting where to dine out.

LIKE INCREASES LIKE

We have said that Ayurveda is an energy-based system. Everything in existence has its unique energetic properties or qualities, including the various foods and each human being. Energies of the same quality add to each other, and too much of any one quality can throw us out of balance. For example, if we feel lethargic, dull, and depressed—all of which are heavy energies—bringing in some movement would help lighten us, as would eating lighter foods such as salads, vegetables, and rice. On the other hand, eating heavier foods such as meat, butter, cheese, and wheat, sleeping more, and being sedentary will exacerbate the problem. If we feel ungrounded, spacey, unable to settle down, all energies that are too light, then activities that ground us, such as digging in the dirt, giving ourselves a foot massage, sitting quietly and paying attention to our breathing, and doing standing yoga poses would be helpful, as would be heavier foods that are grounding and soothing, such as soups and stews.

Ayurveda offers a simple system for balancing the energetic properties of our individual constitution through the foods we eat because it recognizes the connection between the way we feel and our diet and activities. We have far more influence than we think on whether we feel heavy or light, dull or sharp, energetic or lethargic, well or uncomfortable. The next time you experience heartburn, constipation, or dullness in the mind or body, ask yourself what you ate that might have been the culprit rather than just reaching automatically for an antacid, laxative, or cup of coffee. By paying attention to possible connections between the way you feel and the foods you eat, you will soon learn ways to enhance your sense of wellness.

DIGESTION: THE KEYSTONE TO HEALTH

Digestion is the most crucial bodily process for health and longevity, according to the Ayurvedic system. It converts the foods we eat into base materials for the continuous cellular processes of destruction and regeneration. When food is not properly digested, toxins begin to accumulate. In time the toxic buildup leads to symptoms, and later, illnesses, in the physical body. A white coating on the tongue, for example, is an indicator of toxic buildup in the system, as is overly high cholesterol or bad breath.

Ayurveda pays close attention to the process of elimination to detect digestive problems as they occur. A healthy body has at least one bowel movement a day. The quality of our stools, which should be soft and well formed, offers us important information. Constipation or stools that are too hard are indications that something we ate placed too much stress on our digestive system. It is not unusual to become less able to digest meat, cheese, or other foods as we age. This calls for a change in our diet, not the chronic use of laxatives. It is also important to keep in mind that constipation can be a side effect of certain medications.

SUPPORTING DIGESTION

In order for our digestion to function optimally, we should eat only when we are hungry. This is when our digestion is at its most effective, and the foods we consume are metabolized in an optimal manner, which takes at least four hours. Snacking between meals prevents the previous meal from being completely digested, and therefore contributes to the buildup of toxins. Walking for ten minutes after meals helps digestion.

Ayurveda teaches that our digestion is governed primarily by the heating energy, analogous to our Western digestive enzymes, and that it is important not to douse our digestive fire with water immediately before, during, or after meals. Translated into Western lingo, it is important not to dilute the digestive juices. This principle seriously challenges the American habit of guzzling glasses of ice water at meal time. According to Ayurveda, it is far better to drink water between meals. If you feel it necessary to have water during meals, sip only hot or room-temperature water. Taking sufficient time for meals, paying attention to the eating process, and chewing food so thoroughly that it almost turns into liquid assists the digestive process.

Ayurveda also pays attention to food combinations as a way to facilitate digestion. Because our digestive system is not equipped to completely digest two heavy foods simultaneously, it helps to avoid eating concentrated protein with heavy starch, a combination that is common in the Western diet. The Western way of looking at this is that protein and starch require two different enzymes for their digestion. Ayurveda also recommends that we eat only one or two starches at any meal, and that we not mix different kinds of protein, such as meat and milk. Digesting multiple starches or proteins at once hinders the digestive process and compromises absorption and assimilation. In short, eat simply.

Fruits digest easily into their constituent carbohydrates, which monopolize the digestive system and leave the more complex carbohydrates, proteins, and fats in the stomach to putrefy. Ayurveda recommends that most fruits be eaten alone, especially fruits in the melon family. Fruit makes an ideal breakfast or light snack for a person with low blood sugar.

EXERCISE
Exercise relieves stress and supports digestion. That being said, it is important to clarify that not all exercise is equally beneficial. The Western approach to exercise tends toward too much aggression. We believe in no pain, no gain, and we carry exercise to the extreme. A bodybuilder who once wandered into one of my yoga classes was so hindered by the bulk of the very muscles he had taken such pains to build that he was literally unable to stand with his feet separated beyond hip width apart, could not bend forward to touch his toes, nor could he move with any degree of fluidity. The Western approach also tends to view exercise as something to get through rather than experience in our body. I see people reading, listening to headphones, or watching TV while they use treadmills or exercise bikes. This tuning out not only renders them more injury-prone, but also prevents them from developing more awareness of their body and their mind.

Exercising moderately and mindfully, such as doing yoga with the attention focused on the breath and on bodily sensations, is far more stress-relieving than over-stressing the body or exercising with the mind tuned out. An added benefit of exercising mindfully is an increased sense of connectedness with the self. Ayurveda recommends exercising daily. Walking for at least thirty minutes is ideal, especially out of doors. Walk with good posture and be mindful of your surroundings. Try it for a few weeks and see whether you feel more energetic. Obesity is seldom a problem for people in countries where bicycles are still used as a primary means of transportation; and those who live in metropolitan areas and rely on public transportation have the advantage of walking being built into their daily routines.

Doing some yoga daily is also important. Yoga movements lubricate our joints, bring nutrients to our spinal discs, and keep our body supple and youthful. Even after an injury, gentle and appropriate movement frequently helps prevent adhesions from forming and facilitates healing. When we encounter stress, certain muscles tense up and sometimes do not release that tension 100 percent, even after the stress is over. Over time, these contractions build as we become less aware of them, and we eventually forget how to release them consciously. We see examples of this in people whose shoulders are chronically near their ears or whose chests are caved in. When asked to release their shoulders down or to lift and open their chest, they are unable to do so. Yoga stretches help release chronic tension and avoid a daily accumulation of tension.

I have included two sets of yoga stretches at the end of this chapter and a third set of yoga movements at the end of Chapter 9. They can be practiced alone or together. Regular yoga practice will keep your body in good structural balance. It is beneficial to also participate in a yoga class where you can learn correct alignment for the poses to prevent injury and reap the maximum benefit.

Take care to find a qualified instructor. Currently yoga instructors do not have to meet any minimum standards, and many people teaching yoga are not qualified to do so. Teacher-training programs also differ in their thoroughness and quality. Programs can last for a weekend or for several years. However, teachers trained and certified through the Iyengar yoga system have met consistently high standards and are well qualified to instruct. Most importantly, pay attention to your inner experience when you take a class. Ask yourself whether you feel comfortable with the teacher, understand the instructions, and trust that your boundaries will be respected. Your body should feel better and you should feel more energized as well as relaxed after a yoga class—not depleted, exhausted, in pain, or more stressed.

ESTABLISHING A DAILY ROUTINE

Ayurveda teaches that different energies are more prevalent at different times of the day. Therefore, having a daily routine that takes into account the ebb and flow of these cosmic energies means that our activities can be supported by their flow rather than work against them. A regular routine also has a calming effect on us, removing the stress of moment-to-moment decisions, and improves our chances of sustaining good habits.

An ideal routine for the day would begin by rising with the sun. The heavy energies of earth and water prevail from around 6 to 10 a.m. It is important to get moving before that period of time, or else inertia sets in. This is an excellent time for a walk, a run, an active yoga sequence, or any other activity that involves movement. It is also the best time for cleansing, elimination, and an early breakfast, if you are hungry. Even those who describe themselves as not being morning persons will find over time that they feel more energetic during the day if they rise early, as long as they have had sufficient sleep. Lingering in bed, on the other hand, promotes lethargy and inertia. This is something that we can verify for ourselves by paying attention to the relationship between how we start our mornings and how we feel during the day. The active yoga sequence at the end of this chapter is an excellent way to start the morning.

Fire energy, which governs digestion as well as the intellect, is most prominent between 10 a.m. and 2 p.m. Sometime around noon is best for the main meal of the day. Eat your heavy foods then, so they can be properly digested and assimilated. Having meals around the same time each day helps save the body from the stress of constantly adjusting to something new. This is also the best period for tasks that require thinking.

Eat a light dinner before 7 p.m. and avoid eating anything else afterward. Snacking late at night does not allow sufficient time for food to be properly digested; it also contributes to toxic buildups that threaten our health and harm our sleep patterns. Spend the evening quietly. The restorative yoga poses from Chapter 3 are excellent for quieting our body in preparation for sleep.

It is important to be in bed and ready to sleep by 10 p.m. The heavy energies of earth and water prevail again from around 6 to 10 p.m. and support sleep, while the fire energy takes over from around 10 p.m. to 2 a.m. and can interfere with restful sleep. The phenomenon referred to as catching a "second wind" around midnight is a manifestation of the fire energy peaking.

Some people who are used to staying up late believe they function better at night and call themselves night persons. Ayurveda would see them as people who are out of synch with the rhythms of nature.

THE NASAL RINSE

Ayurveda recommends a variety of ways to cleanse the body. The one practice I have found most useful is the nasal rinse. A special vessel is used, called a "neti pot," which resembles a gravy boat. Place a quarter of a teaspoon of sea salt or rock salt in the vessel, and add lukewarm water that feels comfortable to your touch. Lean over the sink, with your head turned to the right, and place the spout against the right nostril. Allow the water to enter the right nostril and tip your head to allow the water to exit through the left nostril. Stop when half the water is used, turn toward the sink and blow through the right nostril to eliminate residual water. Repeat this procedure on the left side. This irrigates the sinus cavities. Any burning sensation most likely means not enough salt is being used. Fifteen to twenty minutes after the rinse, bend over as though you were going to tie your shoes and allow any remaining water to flow out. Do this on an empty stomach.

My husband, who used to suffer at least three serious sinus infections each spring, has been symptom-free since he began using the nasal rinse. It can also help ease allergic reactions to seasonal pollen, the effects of air pollution, and congestion during the winter months. I also use it to prevent my nasal passages from becoming overly dry in heated rooms or desert environments, followed by a couple of drops of nasal oil in each nostril after I have expelled all the water from the nasal cavity. If you notice any signs of cold or infection, you can add to the nasal rinse water a few drops of golden seal tincture, a home-opathic remedy with antibiotic properties. Both the neti pot and the nasal oil can be purchased through suppliers of Ayurvedic products. The neti pot is not the same as saline nasal sprays, which do not irrigate the sinus cavities, and is less invasive than nasal cleansing products in squeeze bottles.

EXERCISE 9—Spinal Health

We are as young as our spine. To keep the spine youthful and supple, it should move daily through the six movements it is capable of doing. Do the following exercise with attention to the sensations in your body and to your breathing. These are good movements to do upon awakening, and a few stretches throughout the day, as needed, keep muscular tension from accumulating. I have given seated versions for numbers 2 and 4 so you can do them at your desk periodically during the workday to prevent or relieve back discomfort.

1. Elongation—Stand in front of a counter, desk, or dresser. Place both hands, shoulder width apart, on the edge of the

counter and step your feet back so your body forms a square with the counter and the floor, with your arms straight. Keep your head between your arms and do not allow it to droop. Now reach your hips away from the counter and allow the movement to lengthen your torso. Experience what it feels like to have the sides of your body getting longer and longer. You will probably feel a concurrent stretch in the backs of your legs. If the sensation in your legs prohibits you from reaching back through the hips, bend your knees slightly. Frequently, lower back pain comes from compression, and this stretch creates space in the spine.

2. Side Bending—Stand with your feet parallel to each other. Press firmly into your feet and extend upward through the crown of your head. With an inhalation, bring your arms overhead, palms facing each other. As you exhale, hold your left wrist with your right hand. Now inhale and grow taller, then exhale and bend toward your right, feeling your left side

stretching. Keep your legs firm. Inhale and come upright; exhale and hold your right wrist with your left hand. Inhale and grow taller, exhale and bend toward your left. Inhale and come upright, exhale and lower your arms to your side. To do this movement while sitting in a chair, be certain to plant your feet firmly on the floor hip width apart and sit upright, balanced on your sitting bones. Do not lean on the back of the chair.

3.   Twist–Sit in an armless chair with your right side toward the back of the chair. Place your feet hip width apart on the floor, directly under your knees. Inhale and lengthen your torso upward. Exhale and turn your belly to the right, toward the back of the chair. Place your hands on the back of the chair. On the next inhalation, lengthen up again and twist a little higher up your spine. You can push into the chair with your right hand and pull with your left to help you rotate along your central axis. Continue to lengthen on the inhale and twist a little higher up your torso on the exhale, finally turning so your right shoulder

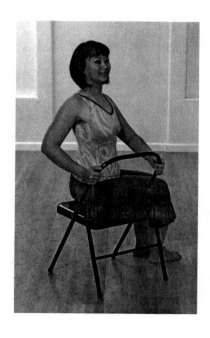

moves backward as your left shoulder moves forward. Inhale and lengthen up one last time, then release the twist on your exhalation, keeping your torso tall. Now sit with your left side facing the back of the chair and repeat to the second side.

4. Cat/Cow–Begin on your hands and knees, with your hands directly under your shoulders, your knees under your hips. Spread your fingers, straighten your arms, and keep them straight. With an exhalation, curl your pelvis in toward your belly. Let your back round like a Halloween cat and your head drop naturally to look at your abdomen. On an inhalation, tilt your pelvis the other way and feel your torso lengthen, your back arch the opposite way; your chest lifts and lengthens forward between your arms. Lead the movements with your pelvis and move your spinal column as a cohesive unit, from your pelvis to the crown of your head, rather than trying to move the different parts of your body separately. Continue these movements five more times, synchronizing them with the breathing pattern given above. This exercise can also be done sitting in a chair, feet firmly on the floor, hip width apart, and ankles under the knees, hands resting on the knees. Again, initiate movement from the pelvis and sense the rest of the spine following accordingly as a unit.

EXERCISE 10–Leg Stretches
This exercise helps to lengthen the hamstrings and open the hips, supporting good posture and back health. It can be added to the earlier exercise for a longer practice. If you don't have a yoga belt, the tie of your bathrobe can serve as a substitute.

1. Lie on your back with your knees bent and your feet on the floor, the belt nearby. Bring your right knee toward your chest and loop the belt around the ball of your right foot, holding the

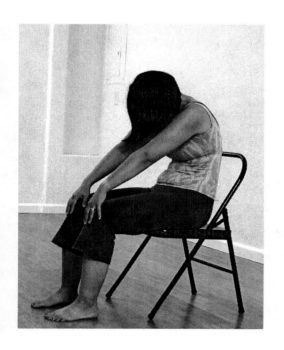 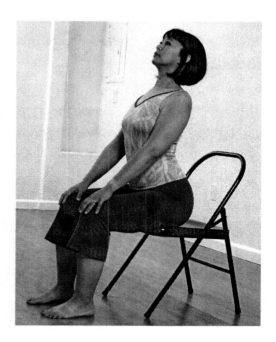

belt with both hands. Lengthen your right leg up toward the ceiling until it is completely straight, pressing through the big toe mound as well as the heel of your right foot. Bring the right shin toward your head to the extent that you can keep the leg straight, while imagining the top of your right thigh moving away from you. Feel the stretch in the back of your thigh and feel your hamstrings lengthen.

2.   Keep the right leg exactly where it is. Slowly lengthen your left leg out along the floor. The stretch in the back of your right leg will intensify as you do this, so pay special attention to keeping the leg straight. Stretch through the left heel and the big toe mound of the left foot and press your upper-left thigh down toward the floor. Keep the legs in this position and continue to breathe smoothly for 20–30 seconds.

3.   Take the belt in your right hand. Keep pressing the left thigh down so the left side of your pelvis remains anchored to the floor. Now slowly release your right leg to the right, to the extent you can do so without the left side of your pelvis leaving the floor. Continue to lengthen through the right heel and breathe smoothly in this position.

4.   Now bring the right leg up to the position in step 2. Take the tie in your left hand and bring the right leg across your body and toward the floor. Keep your right shoulder on the floor but allow the left leg to turn to the left as needed, stretching out through the left heel. Imagine that your right shin is moving toward your left shoulder as your right thigh moves away from you.

5.   Now bring the right leg back up to the position in step 2 again. Release the belt and release your right leg to the floor. Rest and notice how your two legs feel. When you are ready, repeat these steps with your left leg.

SUMMARY

Even though our physical body, with its intricately orchestrated muscular-skeletal system and physiological processes, has an amazing ability to regenerate, it nevertheless requires a certain amount of attention and care to function smoothly. The fast-paced Western lifestyle frequently neglects this preventative aspect. Ayurveda is a holistic system of energy medicine that addresses the cause-and-effect relationship between our diet, lifestyle, and health. An understanding of this relationship expands our options, since there are many things we can do to keep ourselves well. Despite illusions of indestructibility, each of us is gifted with only one life to live, and taking the best possible care of ourselves is the primary way we can express our appreciation for the miracle of our existence. ॐ

Restoring balance to our lives

through nature's rhythms is

the best way to support healthy

sleep habits.

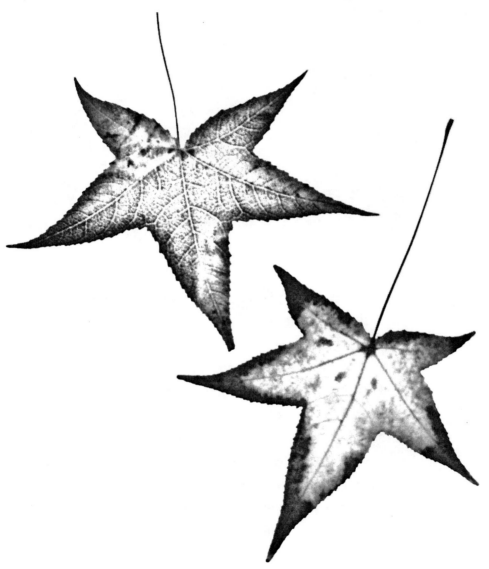

CHAPTER 8

HOW TO SLEEP BETTER

*T*he problem of insomnia has become more common as the level of stress has increased in our society. Most of us experience sleep disturbances at some time in our lives: some people have trouble falling asleep; others wake up in the early hours of the morning and are unable to go back to sleep. An estimated 30–50 percent of the general population experiences sleep disturbances, and for many, the problem has become chronic. Taking a nightly sleeping pill is not a good solution, since the sleep that is induced tends to lack the natural rejuvenating properties. The drug might also have side effects, such as drowsiness and clouded thinking. Developing a dependence on the medication is also a source of concern.

Because restful sleep is essential for the body's renewal and regeneration, this chapter draws on the discussion of Ayurveda in the last chapter and applies that knowledge specifically to the restoration of normal sleep patterns. The practices and abstinences recommended here have been helpful in resolving my own disturbed sleep patterns, which resulted from decades of working late evenings in my psychotherapy practice, and they have also proven helpful for many of my clients and students. Part of this discussion will sound familiar because it recaps material from the last chapter that is pertinent to our present discussion. The exercise at the end of the chapter is a deep relaxation practice, a preparation for restful sleep.

EARLY TO BED AND EARLY TO RISE

Rising with the sun and resting when it sets helps us follow nature's rhythms. Except for a few nocturnal creatures, most animals settle down and rest during the dark hours of the night. True to the methodology of Ayurveda, the best way to regain healthy sleep habits is to restore balance in our lives through a daily routine that is in tune with nature. Going to bed by 10 p.m. at the latest is the key: as explained previously, the restful earth energy that supports sleep recedes after 10 p.m., and the active fire energy, which works against sleep, begins to dominate.

Going to bed before 10 p.m. can be challenging for someone who habitually stays up late. It is impossible to simply go to bed early one night and will ourselves to fall asleep. However, we do have far more control over when we rise in the morning, and that is the better time to initiate change. We can set an alarm and get up earlier, whether or not we feel rested. Avoid taking naps during the day, even if you are tired, so your system has a chance to reset its internal clock. If a nap is unavoidable, keep it short, less than fifteen minutes. Consider making this change slowly but steadily over time.

John, a psychotherapy client, came to me for severe anxiety that resulted from a trauma several years prior. He suffered from many symptoms, one of which was insomnia. John's sleep pattern was completely reversed. He stayed up all night and slept from morning until early afternoon every day. After we resolved some of his more immediate, critical difficulties, John was ready to begin working on establishing a healthier sleep pattern. Despite his fear that he would not be able to function, he decided to set his alarm two hours earlier the next week. To his surprise, he functioned quite well once he dragged himself out of bed. He set his alarm clock another two hours earlier the following week, eventually turning his sleep pattern around after four weeks of diligently working on the problem. John felt more rested during the day as a result of this change, and this positive outcome served as the impetus for him to initiate other constructive changes in his life.

DOS AND DON'TS FOR RESTFUL SLEEP
Besides resetting our internal clocks with the goal of moving bedtime before 10 p.m., there are many other actions we can take to improve the quality of our sleep. Because Ayurveda considers sleep problems to be the result of too much of the moving and unsettling air energy in our system, it urges us to ground ourselves in a consistent daily routine to regain stability and equilibrium. Avoid deviating from this routine on weekends, if at all possible.

Light to moderate exercise, done with mindfulness, grounds us in our body and counteracts sleep disturbances. Avoid anything too strenuous. Walking is excellent, especially when you focus on your feet rolling on the ground as you walk. With swimming, you can concentrate on the movement of your limbs as they propel your body through the water.

Because everything has its own vibration, our surroundings affect us more powerfully than we might think. The bedroom needs to be a calm, tranquil space that promotes relaxation. Keep it neat and tidy, with your bed made daily; an orderly room is soothing for the nervous system. Be aware of how various colors affect you, and make sure that the colors of the walls and artwork in the room are pleasing and calming to you. Your bedroom should be well ventilated and on the cool side, but without cold air blowing directly on you. Do not conduct business or have disturbing conversations in your bedroom, and move the TV elsewhere in the house. Situating the bed so that the head is oriented toward the north or east can be helpful because the energies from those directions are more calming and conducive for sleeping.

Make sure that your bed is comfortable for your body. Aches and pains disturb sleep. Many of my friends gasp when they learn how much I paid for my mattress, but I can't think of any other item in my house that is more important for my well-being than my bed. Also, make sure that your pillows are not so full or stiff that they create neck tension. Select bedding with colors and textures that are pleasing and calming for you.

Allow plenty of time for transitions between activities during the day, and carry that through to bedtime by beginning preparation for sleep by 9 p.m. We prepare babies and young children for bed with a quieting routine, and we need to do the same for ourselves. A soothing bedtime routine might include a warm bath, applying lotion or warm oil to your body, listening to calming music, or using aromatherapy in the form of a scented candle, oil, or stick of incense. Massaging the feet with warm oil before bedtime promotes restful sleep for some people, as does rubbing a couple of drops of lavender oil on the forehead.

Sleep comes naturally and spontaneously when our nervous system is calm. Therefore, what stimulates the nervous system is best avoided and replaced by what is quieting and soothing. All stimulants such as coffee, caffeinated tea, chocolate, highly spiced foods, and carbonated soft drinks should be avoided throughout the day. If this feels impossible, then at least abstain from them from noon onward and work toward total abstinence. Frequently, the longer we abstain, the fewer cravings we experience. Alcohol, an irritant and a depressant, should also be avoided. Even though alcohol sometimes has the effect of inducing drowsiness, it does not encourage natural sleep patterns, and over time damages our health. Many drugs, over-the-counter or prescription, contain stimulants. If you are on medication, it would be wise to check and see whether disturbed sleep might be one of the side effects.

TV, even a pleasant TV program, stimulates our senses and is best avoided in the evenings. This is a tall order for the average American. You might try switching the TV off for a couple of weeks and notice whether you really miss it, or whether it is simply another habit. At the least, avoid programs containing violence or suspense during the evening, and turn the TV off by 9 p.m. It is far better to do gentle yoga stretches, enjoy light reading, listen to pleasant music, sit in the garden with a loved one, or relax in the restorative yoga postures at the end of Chapter 3.

Avoid eating a heavy evening meal, and above all, do not eat after 7 p.m. Otherwise, the body will be straining to digest the food, which works against settling down for sleep. Eat foods that are moist and warm, such as soups, pasta, hot cereals, and vegetable stews. Avoid drying foods such as popcorn or heavy foods such as beef. If you truly feel hungry after 7 p.m., drink some warm milk or broth, but avoid other snacks. I have noticed an increase in disturbing dreams and frequent awakenings when I eat late at night or eat too much for dinner. You can pay attention and notice for yourself the quality of your sleep in relationship to what and how late you eat. Also, taking a ten-minute stroll after your evening meal is not only relaxing but aids digestion.

PRACTICE DETACHMENT

After suffering from insomnia for a while, we can become our own worst enemy. We develop negative internal dialogues and frighten ourselves, such as when we imagine we will be unable to function the next day without sleep. In actuality, most of us function sufficiently well despite suffering from a lack of sleep, and this internal dialogue is simply another manifestation of a negative thinking pattern we discussed earlier. Worrying about not being able to sleep keeps us awake and perpetuates the problem. Some people get up and do other things when they can't sleep. That compounds the problem, because it reinforces the schedule you do not want. Even worse is to get up and eat something, although drinking hot milk does help some people go back to sleep.

A far more effective strategy is to avoid becoming attached to the idea of actually falling asleep. You can actually get by on much less sleep than you might think and still function very well. Understand that just lying in bed quietly resting is good enough. You can selectively focus your attention and notice the smoothness of the sheets, the feeling of cuddling into your bedding and pillows, or simply being aware of your breathing. Do not allow your mind to get into an anxious dialogue about not sleeping and all the imagined dire consequences. Remember, your mind cannot tell imagination from reality, and this kind of anxious thinking interferes with your rest. Anytime you get distracted by your mind, gently bring your attention back to your breathing and bodily sensations. John, in the example above, had to utilize his entire self-calming repertoire to change his sleep schedule, including breath awareness, imagery, meditation, and selective focusing.

Any kind of focus on your breath and bodily sensations in place of thinking is conducive to restful sleep. The following is a deeply relaxing exercise that can be used to stop fretting about not being able to fall asleep.

EXERCISE 11—Deep Relaxation

You can do this exercise in bed in preparation for sleep. Read the instructions several times, and become familiar with the pathway your awareness travels through your body. It is not necessary to be 100 percent accurate. Or you may want to record the instructions, speaking slowly in a soothing tone and pausing after naming each body part. Then play the recording back for yourself so you can relax completely for the exercise. You are free to fall asleep anytime during the exercise.

1.   Lie on your back, with a pillow under your head. Make sure the pillow is thick enough so that the back of your neck is long and your chin does not tilt up toward the ceiling. You can also have a pillow or rolled blanket under your knees if that gives you greater comfort.

2.   Close your eyes, relax your body, and notice your breathing. Notice the room around you, sensing the objects, sounds, and smells. Notice the coolness of the sheets against your skin, the softness of the support under your head, and the back of your body resting on the bed. If thoughts intrude into your consciousness, acknowledge them and put them aside for now, perhaps on the bed next to you.

3.   For the next ten breaths or so, take a nice, gentle, smooth inhalation, then exhale slowly, extending the exhalation without straining. Rest for a few breaths after you finish.

4.   You will now attend to a sequence of certain points on your body. Become aware of each body part as your awareness travels there, then pass on to the next: the space in the center of your forehead and between your eyebrows, the hollow of your throat, your right shoulder joint, right elbow, right wrist, tip of the right thumb, tip of the second finger, third finger, fourth finger, little finger, right wrist, right elbow, right shoulder, hollow of your throat, left shoulder, left elbow, left wrist, tip of your left thumb, second finger, third finger, fourth finger, little finger, left wrist, left elbow, left shoulder, hollow of your throat, your heart center, right nipple, heart center, left nipple, heart center, solar plexus, navel center, right hip, right knee, right ankle, big toe, second toe, third toe, fourth toe, little toe, right ankle, right knee, right hip, navel center, left hip, left knee, left ankle, big toe, second toe, third toe, fourth toe, little toe, left ankle, left knee, left hip, navel center, solar plexus, heart center, hollow of your throat, the space in the center of your head and between your eyebrows.

5.   Now pay attention to the breath in your abdomen and count your breaths backward, from twenty-seven to one: Twenty-seven, belly rising; twenty-seven, belly falling; twenty-six, belly rising; twenty-six, belly falling; and so forth. If you lose count, start over with twenty-seven.

6.   Once you have finished counting the twenty-seven breaths in the abdomen, repeat two more times if you are still awake, once resting on the right side of your body and once on the left. Then relax and breathe gently as you enjoy settling back into the comfort of your bed. Rest quietly there, or repeat any part of this exercise.

SUMMARY

The prevalent use of sleeping aids in society today makes it easy to forget that we can regain normal sleep naturally. The natural way draws on many of the skills we have learned and helps to restore a healthy sleep pattern and overall balance. Give the suggestions in this chapter a try, and see for yourself how they can work for you. Have patience, be gentle with yourself, and avoid frightening yourself with alarmist thoughts. Remember you are a self-regulating being. Trust that once you remove the roadblocks, your natural sleep patterns will be restored. &

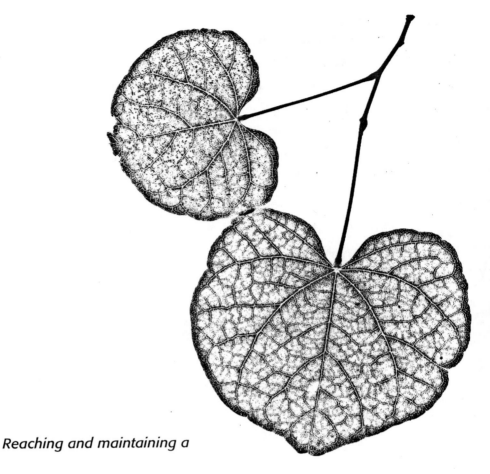

Reaching and maintaining a

weight that is healthy for us

means changing our

relationship to food, our diet,

and our lifestyle.

CHAPTER 9

LOSE WEIGHT AND KEEP IT OFF

*B*esides insomnia, obesity is another escalating health problem in America, affecting even our children, as our lives become more harried and out of synch with nature. Being overweight damages our total being. On a physical level, excess weight places undue stress on our muscular-skeletal system, overtaxes our cardiovascular system, and makes us more susceptible to chronic conditions such as diabetes and hypertension. More subtly, struggling with excess weight diminishes our sense of vitality and aliveness, harms our self-image, and compromises our self-esteem and psychological well-being.

Excess weight also shortens our life span. An overweight ninety-year-old person is a rarity; people blessed with longevity generally seem to be of normal or slightly-below-normal weight. Researchers supported by the National Institute on Aging recently predicted that the average American life span will decrease by as much as five years as a result of obesity. This is the first time in modern history that the younger generation will have shorter and less healthy lives than their parents.

Because of its prevalence and the high risks it poses for our health, excess weight is a topic that, like disturbed sleep, warrants a separate discussion and a more detailed application of the Ayurvedic principles and practices we have learned. Allow any repetition of the material in this new context to be a vehicle for deepening your understanding of the subject matter. We will discuss the relationship between stress and overeating, the importance of self-acceptance in weight management, and specific tools for changing our eating habits for the better.

STRESS AND WEIGHT

It is well established that people eat to relieve stress. If our lives have become more stressful, it stands to reason that obesity has also become a more prevalent problem. A recent study on the aftermath of stress found that the subjects who were stressed snacked twice as much on foods with a high fat content than the subjects who were not as stressed, even after the stressful event was well over. The effects of stress are longer lasting than we might think, and prolonged stress can turn maladaptive attempts at stress relief into self-injurious habits.

I find the increasing incidence of excess weight in children particularly alarming because being overweight in childhood predisposes the individual to obesity in adulthood. The answer to this problem is not to sue McDonalds, but to examine our culture more closely and take stock of how our own behavior might have been influenced. Children undergo an inordinate amount of stress. Achievement is demanded of them in kinder-garten, if not in preschool, and the best schools have become synonymous with those that have the highest test scores and the highest admission rates to desirable colleges. Absent are the concurrent considerations: emotional factors, such as whether the schools also help children feel safe, comfortable, nurtured, and supported in their individuality; and health factors, such as whether the meals offered are nutritious and healthy.

As children spend more time alone because their parents are

working longer hours, they have to rely on their own psycho-logical resources more than is beneficial. As parents become preoccupied with their own stress, they may not have as much time or patience to just listen. Children feel their parents' emotional disengagement even though they may not be able to put their feelings into words, and overeating is a common way to try to alleviate loneliness and boredom. Also, because families have less available time, they eat out more often, consuming fat-laden foods in larger quantities, and doing so later in the evening. Mealtime is likely to be one more thing to hurry through, rather than an occasion for the family to come together and share their experiences.

Since our whole society is geared toward achievement, it is diffi-cult for parents to avoid getting caught up in their children's accomplishments, and home might become one more source of pressure for children rather than their refuge. We want to give our children the best, but our cultural values make it easy to forget that children's needs are simple. Like adults, their essen-tial need is for a relaxed sense of belonging within the safety of a supportive family. It is important we do not confuse this need with enrichment, such as lessons in music, dance, and sports.

BODY IMAGE AND WEIGHT

The concept of the ideal body shape, especially for women, has changed with time. Looking at paintings from earlier eras, we see feminine shapes that are soft, slightly plump, with curvy hips and developed breasts. The ideal body shape in our contemporary society, however, has become more androgy-nous. Slim, masculine hips, lean, long lines, and less-developed breasts are now in vogue. This description fits the shape of girls in their teens rather than that of most mature women. At the same time, our society has become increasingly concerned with how things appear than with their substance. We have indeed come to judge people as well as books by their cover rather than their content.

With the amazing ability of modern media to disseminate information, it is difficult to not become brainwashed as to how our body should appear. Since most women do not have the body of a young girl, they suffer from some degree of a negative body image and a preoccupation with their appearance. It is not by accident that the last few decades have ushered in the syndrome of life-threatening eating disorders, characterized by a distorted body image and an obsession with thinness. If we were to consider the dynamics behind these illnesses, we would see them as disorders of self-alienation or spiritual crisis resulting from the negation of the true, essential self.

DEFINING HEALTHY WEIGHT
Let us clarify exactly what we are referring to as *healthy* weight. For certain, it is unlikely to be the weight our image-driven society might dictate. True to its individually oriented approach, Ayurveda teaches that each of us has a weight that is ideally suitable. Those of us born with a larger proportion of the heavy earth energy have a heavier and sturdier bone structure, are broader across the hips and shoulders, and naturally weigh more than others of the same height who have a smaller, lighter bone structure and a less-developed physique.

For our purposes then, healthy weight refers to the weight that *feels the best and the most right to us*. In other words, we must turn inward and listen to our internal experiences rather than conform to externally dictated standards. We must notice at what weight we feel the most energetic, vital, and healthy, at what weight we begin to feel thickened, heavy, dull, and uncomfortably large.

SUSTAINABLE WEIGHT LOSS

Ayurveda considers excess weight to be the result of too much earth and water energies in the system. This is why people with a predominance of these energies are particularly vulnerable to weight gain. The way to reach and maintain a healthy weight is by restoring balance to our system. We can accomplish this by following the principle of "like increases like," and reducing our intake of foods that are composed primarily of the earth and water energies.

To counteract the heaviness of earth energy, it is important to stay with a light, primarily plant-based diet. Avoid heavy foods such as animal protein, fat, nuts, sweets, cheese, cream, and foods fried in excess oil. For non-vegetarians, choose white meat such as chicken, turkey, or fish. Also, avoid foods that are very salty or sour, to minimize water retention. Instead, choose lightly dressed salads, soy protein, fresh vegetables, and light grains such as rice, barley, corn, millet, buckwheat, and rye. Choose lighter fruits such as apples and pears, and avoid fruits that are heavier and very sweet, as well as fruits with a high water content, such as bananas, cantaloupes, and watermelons. Choose honey, a natural product, in place of sugar for sweetening; and reduce or eliminate the amount of wheat in your diet.

Establishing a healthy daily routine is equally important when it comes to sustainable weight loss. Remember to eat the main meal at midday, leave at least four hours between meals for food to properly digest, eliminate snacking, and avoid eating after 7 p.m. Depending on the unique blend of the five elemental energies in our body, it is not only acceptable but recommended that some of us delay breakfast until hunger occurs. This is one way Ayurveda differs from most Western nutritional advice. You can tell whether this practice is appropriate for you by noticing how you respond to it. For example, my body has never felt good when I eat early in the day, and it is validating to find a system that gives me permission to skip breakfast. On the other hand, my daughter becomes highly irritable anytime she misses a meal, and a good friend feels ungrounded and flighty if she does not have breakfast. Obviously, this practice is not suitable for either of their energetic compositions, while it is perfect for me.

Because the heavy earth energy is stagnant, we must exercise daily, except during menstruation, for a minimum of 30 minutes to maintain weight, longer to shed excess pounds. Brisk walking is appropriate, as is jogging and swimming. I have included instructions for Salutations to the Sun at the end of this chapter. Build up slowly but steadily in terms of the number of repetitions. Starting the day with these yoga movements counteracts the heavy earth energy, vitalizes you, and exercises all your joints and muscle groups. Regular yoga practice not only increases energy, but also develops body awareness and concentration so we can better monitor our sensations of hunger or satiation, the importance of which we will discuss below.

Even though the practice of fasting one day a week is for the purpose of supporting digestion and not for weight loss, losing weight is nevertheless a side benefit of weekly fasts, and good digestion in turn supports weight loss. It is important, however, that we do not abuse this practice for the purpose of shedding weight. As stated above, if you decide to try this practice, spend the day of fasting quietly in contemplation and avoid overly exerting yourself. It is important to drink plenty of water to stay hydrated. My own version of this practice is to drink cups of hot water, herbal tea, or liquefied vegetable soup when I experience hunger. It is important not to feel deprived during our day of fasting.

SATIATION SCALE

If we eat only when we are truly hungry and stop eating when we feel full, we will naturally arrive and remain at a weight that is healthy for us. In order to eat only until we are full, we need to decipher the cues our stomach gives us. Because many of us have lost touch with the sensations that tell us we have eaten enough, the scale below is useful for re-educating ourselves. To use the scale effectively, it is necessary to devote our undivided attention to our eating, at least in the beginning, until we become familiar with our bodily cues in terms of when we are hungry and when we are full. This means we do not read, watch TV, or chat with a friend during our meals.

0............1............2............3............4............5............6............7
   starved begin   pay   stop   stuffed
            eating   attention

0–1   Stomach has long been empty and is growling.
      Eat before this.
1–2   Stomach is empty, beginning sensations of hunger.
      Begin to eat.
2–4   Stomach is comfortable while eating. *Continue eating.*
4–5   Beginning feelings of fullness. *Pay careful attention.*
5–6   Feeling full and satisfied. *Stop eating.*
6–7   Feeling stuffed, heavy, uncomfortable. *Gone too far!!*

As you can see, you are asked to avoid getting overly hungry. When we get to that point, we are putting ourselves at risk for binging. People who consistently alternate between starving and binging suffer from an eating disorder. Because the difference between feeling satisfied and overly full can be a matter of just two or three bites, it is important to eat slowly and pay attention to the sensations. Eating according to our feelings of hunger and satiation is a lifelong practice that will help us keep our weight at a level that is healthy for us.

FOOD & FEELINGS DIARY
I have had people tell me that they eat next to nothing and yet they still cannot shed any weight. This cannot be true. It is not that they are lying; many people are simply not cognizant of the amount of food they consume. They might remember eating three reasonably sized meals one day, but forget that they also had a large piece of birthday cake at work or a cup of hot chocolate while visiting a friend, in addition to a handful of peanuts as they passed a coworker's desk. This is why it is essential that we keep a food diary when we decide to change our eating habits. Every single bite of food we put into our mouth is to be recorded in the diary. A food diary promotes awareness, and it is important to eat as the result of conscious choice. Many people are surprised to learn how much they unconsciously pop into their mouths throughout the day; others have reported that the trouble of having to write it down deterred them from snacking.

Overeating is frequently an unconscious habit meant to relieve stress, since it helps us avoid difficult feelings. We eat unconsciously and hardly even taste the food. This is why the food diary has a section for feelings and preceding events. Becoming conscious of our feelings and identifying their triggers is particularly pertinent when we have swerved way off our path and binged.

Try to recall the events preceding the episode of overeating, identify the emotions involved, and record them in the sample format below or one similar to it. Examine in detail the emotions that were difficult to tolerate, and consider alternative ways to address the emotions, without food. With a better understanding of what transpired, identify any actions you might need to take at this point to redress the original situation. Taking appropriate action anchors new behavior in our repertoire and increases our immunity to stress. Over time we see a pattern emerge between overeating and the bypassed stressful emotions, and this insight enhances our self-understanding.

Date	Monday, November 18
Time	4:35 p.m.
What I Ate	1/2 bag of corn chips and 4 chocolate chip cookies with 3/4 glass of milk
What Happened Before	Mother-in-law called and told me we will have to host the Thanksgiving dinner because Don's sister just can't deal with the stress right now.
How I Felt About What Happened	Angry to be dumped on again. Hurt that Don has trouble sticking up for us. Anxious about cooking a dinner that will be good enough. Stressed at having one more thing to do.
Strategies Other Than Eating	Remember next time to tell her I'll think about it rather than just acquiescing. Take deep breaths. Call Mary and talk to her about my feelings. I did do that after the 4th cookie and stopped eating. Next time maybe it'll be sooner.
Anything to do for Closure?	Call mother-in-law back and tell her that the dinner will be a potluck this year, and tell her what I need her to bring. Also change the time from 3 to 5 p.m. for people to begin arriving.

MORE STRATEGIES

From my own experience and from working with clients, I've learned that the single most difficult strategy to implement is not eating after 7 p.m. Evenings are when we finally slow down and become aware of our stress and fatigue. Many of us are also more likely to feel lonely in the evenings. To soothe ourselves, we frequently link snacking with other activities, such as watching TV or reading a book. Just like having a cigarette with a cup of coffee, it is difficult for us to engage in one activity without evoking the need to engage in the other, once the link has been established. To avoid eating after 7 p.m., it is critical that we break the association between eating and other activities. When it is time to eat, sit down, eat slowly and consciously, and savor the food in quiet surroundings. Postpone the activity that has become associated with eating, and keep it separate. It also helps to develop new and more active habits. You can practice yoga, take a walk, do breathing exercises, meditate, or spend time with people with good energy during the difficult evenings. Other possibilities are to prearrange to call a person you trust, should you experience the urge to snack, or draw on Chapter 6 and use journaling to record your feelings and relate more intimately with your inner self.

NO SHORTCUTS

Weight loss has become a multi-billion-dollar industry. Unfortunately, only a minority of people sustain the weight loss they achieve. This is because Americans have a penchant for quick solutions, such as diet pills, liquid diets, and raw foods. We keep looking to something outside of ourselves to do the work for us. We also tend to choose fad diets that promise quick results but are detrimental to our health, such as the popular Atkins diet, which is high in saturated fat and animal protein, a way of eating that studies have shown puts us at high risk for heart attacks, strokes, gout, and osteoporosis.

While these extreme measures might bring about quick weight loss, they are not ways of eating that are sustainable. We only fool ourselves when we believe we can achieve permanent weight loss through temporary behavior changes. Once we resume our old habits, we regain the weight we lost. Multiple cycles of weight loss and weight gain actually work against our purposes. Our body cannot tell the reason for these cycles, believes it is facing starvation, and slows our metabolism accordingly, making weight loss increasingly more difficult. There are simply no magical answers when it comes to maintaining our weight at a level that is healthy for us. Our weight is directly related to what, when, and how much we eat, and there is no substitute for changing our relationship to food, our diet, and our lifestyle.

SELF-ACCEPTANCE, PERFECTIONISM, RIGHT MOTIVATION

To successfully shed excess pounds and maintain a weight that is healthy for us, we need the backdrop of an accepting, nonjudgmental attitude toward ourselves. We must accept our unique body composition and shed our preconceived ideas about how we should look. Instead, let our primary motivation for weight loss be that of restoring balance to our system, keeping ourselves healthy, and maximizing our sense of ease, vitality, and aliveness. If our sole purpose is to lose weight for the sake of our appearance, we are less likely to succeed, since it is more difficult to bring our total being, body and soul, into accord behind a goal that is ego-driven rather than one that is of intrinsic benefit to us.

Do not expect yourself to be perfect in eating healthfully. Numerous projects of self-improvement have been truncated because of perfectionism. How many of us have embarked on a healthy eating plan but abandoned ship as soon as we wandered off-track? Consider the following scenario: we eat something we shouldn't, we see this as our whole plan being ruined, we feel bad, we tell ourselves it no longer matters so we might as well really go on a binge, we binge eat, we feel even worse, and so on and so forth. Might this be a familiar thought pattern and vicious cycle? Wouldn't it be much better to just get back on track? Remember that it is not the occasional hamburger but the ongoing poor dietary habits that put us at risk. Be gentle with yourself, and far more constructively, pay attention to the circumstances, feelings, thoughts, and experiences that preceded going off-track through the Food & Feelings Diary.

EXERCISE 12—Salutations to the Sun

This is a more active practice that can stand alone, or it can follow Exercises 9 and 10 for a longer practice. It efficiently works every muscle group in the body and lubricates the joints. Move slowly, with awareness of your bodily sensations and synchronize the movements with your breathing. Do not strain. Do a minimum of two rounds, building up slowly over time to twelve. Pay close attention to your energy level and avoid overexertion. Allow two hours after eating before doing this exercise.

1.   Stand with the outer edges of your feet parallel, your weight balanced over your feet, hands together in a prayer position, and breathe evenly for a few rounds.

2.   With an inhalation, bring your arms overhead, palms facing each other, stepping strongly into your feet as you extend your torso upward, keeping your chest lifted.

3.   With an exhalation, hinge forward at the hips and bring your hands to the floor, shoulder width apart and under your shoulders. You can rest your hands lightly on your shins if they do not reach the floor. You can also bend your knees slightly if you need to.

4.   With an inhalation, keep your hands on the floor, bend your left knee and step your right foot back, resting your right knee on

the floor and bringing your hips forward and down. Your right thigh should be at a diagonal with the floor, and your left knee should be directly over your left ankle, not in front of it. You will likely feel a stretch in the front of your right thigh. Keep your shoulders over your hips and bring your arms overhead, palms facing each other and elbows straight.

5. With an exhalation, bring your hands down to the floor, shoulder width apart. Spread your fingers and firm your arms. Lift your right knee and step your left foot back to be hip width apart from your right foot. Push your shoulders and hips back and your buttocks up so your body makes an inverted V shape. Move your thighs back strongly to relieve pressure in your wrists. If that is not possible due to tightness in the backs of your legs, you can bend your knees slightly. You can rest here for a few breaths if you wish.

6. With an exhalation, bring both knees to the floor, bend your elbows, keep them in toward each other along your torso, and lower your torso to the floor to lie face down on the floor.

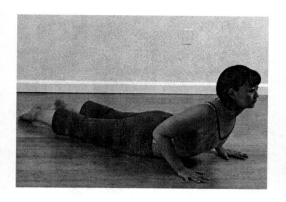 

7. With an inhalation, bring your chest forward and up, using your hands for support. Allow your head to follow naturally as part of your spine.

8. With an exhalation, spread your fingers, strengthen your arms, come to your knees, and push yourself back into the same inverted V as in step 5.

9. With an inhalation, bring your left knee to the floor and your right foot forward. This is similar to step 4, except now it is your right ankle you have to make certain is directly below the right knee. Keep your shoulders over the hips and bring your arms up toward the ceiling, palms facing each other.

10. With an exhalation, step into your right foot and bring your left foot forward next to it, as in step 3. Straighten your legs with your chest close to your thighs if you can, or bend your knees slightly.

11. With an inhalation, step strongly into your feet and bring your torso upright, extending upward, with your arms over your head, as in step 2.

12. With an exhalation, bring your hands into a prayer position as in step 1, standing tall. Breathe slowly and mindfully for a few rounds before repeating the set of movements.

13. When you have finished, lie down on your back and relax your body onto the ground. Close your eyes and place your eye pillow over them if you have one. Your can place a rolled blanket or pillow under your thighs if that feels better for your back. Breathe lightly and allow your mind to relax completely. Stay here for at least five minutes so your body can integrate the practice you just finished; ten minutes is even better.

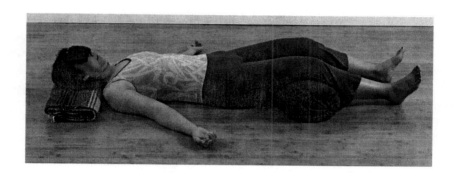

SUMMARY

Obesity is anticipated to become America's number-one killer. It predisposes us to a plethora of life-threatening illnesses. Not only will our children's generation have a shorter life span as a result of this problem, but the increased need for medical care will create a financial burden that our society is ill-prepared to address. Even though obesity is now being recognized as a public health issue, weight management is really an individual responsibility. This chapter has addressed the direct relationship between weight and dietary habits. It is only when we accept that there are no shortcuts and become willing to make the necessary adjustments in our diet and lifestyle that maintaining a healthy weight is possible. ❧

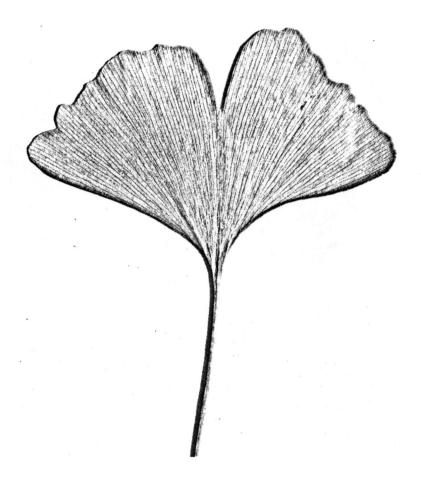

Kindness, compassion, tolerance, and collaboration

provide the foundation for satisfying relationships.

CHAPTER 10

FINAL INGREDIENTS FOR LOW-STRESS LIVING

We have developed an understanding of the dynamics of stress, and we have explored ways to recognize and counteract it on many levels. We know that a healthy diet, regular exercise, and a daily routine that is in synch with nature's rhythms promotes wellness. We can rely on conscious breathing to keep ourselves calm and focused. We understand the importance of limiting stimulation and the need for regular rest. We have tools to manage difficult emotions, identify and release fear-driven behavior patterns, and recognize and let go of negative thought patterns. We have explored the benefits of giving more credence to our internal experiences in order to establish a better balance between our intellect and intuition. And we recognize the critical role self-acceptance plays in deepening our self-understanding and making positive changes.

This final chapter addresses the important role that loving relationships, ethical values, and contentment play in creating a low-stress lifestyle. These life elements compose the backdrop for how we perceive ourselves and how we relate to others. Because each of these subjects constitutes a whole field of study, our discussion here is necessarily introductory in nature, with the objective of bringing awareness and evoking thought, the first steps toward change. Implement some of the suggestions and experience their beneficial effects for yourself. Awareness exercises are included to make the material more personally pertinent. You can do these exercises later or as you read along, but do allow ample quiet time for reflection. For those who want to delve more deeply into these matters, suggestions for further reading are included at the end of the book.

LOVING RELATIONSHIPS

Just as a healthy diet and a daily routine that flows in rhythm with nature are essential ingredients for physical health, harmonious relationships and a sense of community are crucial elements for emotional well-being. Our essential nature seeks unity and oneness with all things. The need to love and be loved is innate. We experience stress when we are in conflict with others. A quarrel with a mate, harsh words with a colleague, a misunderstanding with a friend, or even an unpleasant interaction with a complete stranger can haunt us for days or longer. For the same reason, a prolonged sense of isolation depresses the spirit. Studies have shown that people with loving relationships, even when that relationship is with a pet, survive stressful events better than those living in isolation.

Yet it is easy to take our loved ones for granted. Just as our senses can dull with overstimulation, proximity and familiarity over time can dull our relational awareness. We might assume we already know what the other person is saying, so we stop listening. We may no longer notice how we sound and behave with the people we are close to. It is easy to fall into the habit of taking the expedient way out rather than doing what is necessary or right. Or we might simply get lost in the minutiae of day-to-day living and forget that relationships need nurturing.

Besides this natural tendency to drift into apathy about our relationships, misinformation can also be a problem. I have had a surprising number of clients in relationship counseling say that they believed they could let go of the niceties once a relationship was established. Many also acknowledge that they tend to give more consideration to strangers and acquaintances than they do to their families. This is unfortunate because in actuality, people who care about us are more deeply affected by our actions than strangers are, and therefore require more consideration from us, not less. And no matter how secure or comfortable we become in a relationship, courtesy and mutual respect are necessary ingredients for the relationship to remain satisfying.

The nurturing of relationships is often dictated by Father Time. Children grow up, parents die, friends and spouses need us more at certain times than others. If we are unavailable during these critical times, we have missed an opportunity, since life experiences cannot be re-created. In fact, people who are at the end of their lives frequently express the wish that they had been more loving, patient, generous, understanding, or forgiving, or that they had spent more quality time with the people who mattered to them. Seldom do they wish they had made more money, won more competitions, or worked longer hours. As a personal illustration, I belatedly realized that I did not fully appreciate the joys of parenting when my children were young. Due to a variety of reasons, I was often harried and not fully present. Those little people now exist only in my memory, and it is with much sadness that I acknowledge that I missed out on consciously living and savoring a whole segment of my life.

Even though we cannot change the past, we can practice self-forgiveness and be mindful of how we allocate the precious resources of our time and energy now, to avoid sowing seeds for future regrets. Many people were surprised when I decided to drive 350 miles round-trip each week for four months to spend an afternoon with a grandchild who needed company during that period of time. I was not being a martyr, nor was I doing penance for all the times I fell short in my parenting of his mother. My primary motivation was to make the most of an opportunity to enjoy a dear little person before he also metamorphosed into an adult.

Periodically re-examining the way we prioritize our time and energy helps keep our awareness keen. A friend of mine makes this kind of re-evaluation an annual ritual for herself, usually on New Year's Eve. She spends some time in reflection on the year that has passed, followed by setting new intentions for the year to come.

There are many things we can do to improve a relationship, whether or not the other person joins us in this endeavor. Though our tendency is to want the other person to be different, it is important to remember that people are usually doing the best they can. Frequently there can be a vast improvement when we stop adding our piece of fuel to the fire. Improving others is not our job. Our job is to practice tolerance and forgiveness, and to manage our own thoughts, beliefs, emotions, motivations, and behavior. The following example happens to be about a parent-child relationship. Many of my client's marriages have improved through similar processes, even though their spouses were not involved in therapy with them.

Joy consulted me because she wanted to improve her relationship with her mother. Their times together frequently ended in arguments and hurt feelings. Joy would talk to her mother about something for which she needed her mother's support and understanding. Instead, her mother would give her advice and sometimes even minimize Joy's feelings. As Joy's therapy progressed, she began to understand that her mother became anxious when Joy expressed emotional discomfort. The advice-giving, therefore, was not due to her mother's lack of confidence in Joy's ability to handle her life, as Joy had believed. Instead, it was her mother's way of trying to soothe Joy so she could allay her own anxiety. Joy's new perspective freed her from a repetitive negative dialogue with her mother. Instead of looking to her mother for what she could not provide, Joy joined a therapy group that gave her the emotional support she needed. When she spent time with her mother, Joy actively guided their conversations to emotionally neutral topics they both enjoyed discussing.

AWARENESS EXERCISE

Sit quietly and take some calming breaths. Without self-recrimination, think of the people in your life one at a time, and consider how you relate to them. Take a little time with each question before moving on to the next one. Do you spend quality time with them? Do you listen carefully to what they say and understand what they might need from you, or do you habitually rush in with unsolicited advice or judgment, or listen with only half an ear? Do you speak to them courteously? Do you respect their feelings even though you may not agree with them? Are you likely to be less patient and less tolerant with your intimates than you are with strangers? Would you want your friends, colleagues, or mate to treat you as you treat them? What are some of the ways you might relate better with the people you love?

VALUES, INTEGRITY, AND SELF-ESTEEM

Closely related to the subject of relationships is that of ethical values, which have suffered a dramatic decline in our society over the last few decades. We no longer emphasize the foundational qualities that sustain human relationships, such as patience, tolerance, empathy, compassion, kindness, generosity, honesty, mutuality, loyalty, and the willingness to occasionally set our own needs aside. Integrity or a personal code of behavior upon which we and others can rely has also become a rare phenomenon, whether in business, politics, or personal relationships. As a result, we lack what it takes to sustain relationships through the vicissitudes of life. It is difficult not to see a correlation between the erosion of these values and the escalation of the divorce rate—one measure of relationship satisfaction—to an astonishing 50 percent or more.

Even more importantly, ethical values and a sense of integrity are the cornerstones of genuine self-esteem because these qualities constitute our true nature. Being compassionate, kind, and generous is our natural state before fear leads us astray. The more we live in congruence with how we were meant to be, the better we feel about ourselves. When we are dishonest, unreliable, aggressive, or in any other way harm others, we violate not only the other person but also our own essential nature. In short, self-esteem depends on how we live in the world, in relationship to all that is around us. We need to know that through our actions, we leave the world a better place as a result of our existence. However much we might be able to project an image of goodness so we can receive others' approval and admiration, our innate intelligence always knows the truth.

I remember clearly the first time I experienced the qualities of compassion and kindness within myself. I had accompanied my youngest child to her first kindergarten class. A young Hispanic girl had accompanied her little sister to the same class, and was trying to tell the teacher that her sister didn't speak English. To my surprise, the same teacher who so reassuringly welcomed my daughter responded brusquely and shut the classroom door in her face. The girl sat down on the curb and burst into tears. Even though I was in my usual hurry and would normally have rushed off, something softened in me and I took the time to sit with her until she felt better. In this seemingly insignificant and, until now, private moment, I caught a glimpse of my essential nature. That moment was part of the impetus for a long journey of self-inquiry and behavior changes that eventually helped me shed a negative self-image.

Over the years I have many times fallen short of the values I hold important. During those times, this and other similar memories help remind me that my essential nature is that of goodness. Look back and remember the times you went out of your way to be kind or generous to someone, not because it was convenient but because you perceived that person's need. Take a moment and notice how you feel about yourself for having done so.

In the absence of a sufficient level of true self-esteem, we come to rely on artificial criteria to establish our worth, such as our appearance, the kind of work we do, our income, and others' good opinion of us. This reliance on external factors separates us even further from our essential goodness and forces us to continuously achieve, please, and look good to convince ourselves of our worth. Our experience of who we are becomes based on a false sense of self that wisdom traditions refer to as "ego," a state of alienation from our essential self. This usage is different from the term "ego" as it is used in psychology.

Having our sense of self based in ego is stress inducing because the way we feel about ourselves is likely to be unstable and fluctuating. We might feel on top of the world one day and worthless the next, since external circumstances are subject to constant changes that are largely out of our control. There is always someone who does more, earns more, or looks better than we do, and whether we please another person depends on that person's unique preferences or immediate mood rather than anything personal about us.

These fluctuating emotions are not only stressful in themselves but can also lead to our behaving in accordance with what makes us look good or feel good rather than what is right. Thus we are more likely to sacrifice integrity in favor of expediency and become less trustworthy. Alienated from our own goodness, we also have more difficulty recognizing true goodness in others, and our ability to recognize trustworthiness in others becomes diminished. Both of these factors increase the likelihood of troubled relationships, leading to further situational stress.

Certain physical factors we might base our worth on are also necessarily transient. A youthful appearance or athletic prowess, for example, fades over time. Unless we can bridge the gap between an ego-based sense of worth and our essential nature, it is difficult to retain a sense of purpose in life, and aging becomes an increasingly difficult process.

AWARENESS EXERCISE

Sit quietly and reflect on the essence of each of the following qualities: patience, tolerance, kindness, generosity, honesty, loyalty, and integrity. Can you recall people you know who embody some or all of these qualities? Spend a little time remembering each of them and notice what it was like to have had him or her touch your life. Now think of people in your life who have been impatient, intolerant, selfish, aggressive, competitive, dishonest, or expedient. How do you feel about them?

Impartially and without judgment, now consider how you are in terms of each of these qualities. For example, are you generally patient? Likely to behave kindly even when you feel annoyed? Tolerant of differences in opinion, cultural traditions, religious and political beliefs? Generous with your time, energy, and good will? Usually able to do what is "right" even though to do so might be more difficult than the alternative? Willing to tell the truth but with tact and without hurting someone in the process? Are you someone you would like to have for a friend?

Remember that these qualities, desirable or not, do not reside in us in an all-or-nothing manner. Positive qualities are already within all of us waiting to be manifested because they are a part of our essential nature.

CONTENTMENT

Contentment is the state of not desiring something other than what we have. It is important to clarify that contentment does not mean we never want anything, care about what happens, make plans for the future, or become passionate about a project. What it does mean is that we are not so intent on these things coming to pass in a specific way that our peace of mind becomes dependent on their outcome. An expanded understanding of contentment also includes a sense of appreciation for, satisfaction with, and gratitude for what we do have.

While contentment might seem similar to happiness at first glance, they are actually different experiences. Happiness has the connotation of excitement or arousal, something outside of us we have to pursue. Contentment suggests a state within us that is simple, calm, stable. Western society accords more importance to the pursuit of happiness, whereas Eastern traditions place more emphasis on the cultivation of contentment. In fact, contentment is one of the essential practices of yoga philosophy.

A sense of contentment forms the backdrop for low-stress living. Not desiring other than what we have takes the focus off of what is lacking and relieves us from the ego-driven need to strive for more, bigger, or better, a vicious cycle that brings no lasting satisfaction. It is a matter of thinking of the glass as half-full rather than half-empty. It is seeing our circumstances as being already complete and everything else as only the frosting. In this way we remove any prerequisites for enjoying life, such as having to first lose weight, get a promotion, buy a new house, or find the right partner. This perspective frees us to appreciate and make the most of the many blessings we do have. It is only when we are content that we can experience gratitude and forgiveness. Paradoxically, it is only when we give up chasing after happiness that we can be in touch with the innate joy that is our true nature.

Contentment enables us to accept our life as it unfolds in its entirety, including the sorrows and joys that are integral parts of any life. This acceptance is especially important as we age. Children leave home; family members and friends become ill or die; our hearing, eyesight, and memory deteriorate; we lose our youthful looks and bearing. If we live long enough, even our children may predecease us. A sense of contentment makes it possible for us to face these and other difficult circumstances with equanimity and still feel satisfied with the totality of our lives. We do not think of losses as personal tragedies, nor face with outrage what is natural to the life process. Instead of becoming increasingly bitter and self-pitying, we can retain a sense of gratitude for the multitude of gifts we retain, foremost of which is the gift of life itself. The ability to achieve such inner peace when things go awry provides a high level of immunity to stress.

It is not unusual for contentment to be heralded by adversity, for adversity tends to alter our perspective. Depending on how we view a situation, the same circumstances can elicit very different responses. As my world was falling apart during my divorce, I overheard a woman angrily complaining that the paint she had purchased was a shade off from what she had had in mind. In that moment I became acutely aware of my own capacity for tunnel vision, for I had been that woman only a few months earlier. The wrong shade of paint, milk being spilt on a freshly mopped floor, or a disruption of vacation plans would invariably throw me off balance. It was only in the throes of far greater misery that I came to understand the comparative insignificance of most difficulties, and this understanding expanded my capacity for contentment.

We can actively cultivate contentment by being more present to our experiences—savoring the simple pleasures inherent in each moment, such as the feel of the sun on our skin, the first bite into a juicy apple, fresh air in our nostrils as we step outdoors, or the experience of affection for someone we love. Regardless of external circumstances, these simple pleasures are always available to us. The times we experience difficulties are excellent opportunities to practice the art of contentment. These are the times when we are called on to consciously expand our perspective so that whatever difficulties facing us can be viewed as part of a larger paradigm in which many things are also going right.

SUMMARY

This chapter discussed some of the philosophical considerations that provide the foundation for a low-stress lifestyle. We talked about the importance of accepting all of life, the joyous and the painful that is inherent in all lives. This acceptance of how life truly is eliminates the futile and stress-inducing struggle against the unavoidable. We said that contentment can be actively cultivated by acknowledging all our precious gifts, including the gift of life itself. Being content with what we have frees us from a rapacious appetite that can never be satisfied. We discussed how living from a personal sense of integrity founded on the values of honesty and the non-harming of others reconnects us with our inherent goodness, which is the foundation for true self-esteem. This unshakable knowledge of our own goodness relieves us of the impossible task of continuously proving our worth. We discussed our innate need for harmonious relationships, the importance of consciously prioritizing our time and energy in congruence with this need, and the role of forgiveness, tolerance, and acceptance toward others as well as ourselves.

These philosophical considerations affect our core beliefs about how life works, who we are, how we relate to others, and our place in the world. Grounded in solid principles, our lives take on meaning and purpose. Without this foundation, we can only use our stress-reducing tools to "put out fires." This is not the same as creating a life that is naturally low in stress.

This last chapter has been difficult to write. There is so much more of value that could have been discussed that the process of deciding what to include and exclude became impossible. In the end, I had to practice what I preached. I put the project aside and stopped thinking. I practiced yoga and meditated for several months before my intuition reawakened and the material poured forth. Like all of life, creativity emerges of its own accord and in its own time. We can but set our intention and bow to the natural process. ❧

A sense of contentment

forms the backdrop for low-stress living.

SUGGESTED RESOURCES

My relaxation CD "Yoga Nidra: Therapeutic Deep Relaxation," published by Fig Garden Press, is available at www.FigGardenPress.com. Yoga Nidra is one of the most effective ways to relax physically, emotionally, and mentally. I encourage you to listen to the whole CD a few times to familiarize yourself with it, and then select specific tracks that are the most soothing to you or that best fit into the time you have available.

CHAPTER 1—What Stress is and How it Works
- Robert M. Sapolsky, *Why Zebras Don't Get Ulcers*, W. H. Freeman & Company, New York, 1994
One of my references on the physiology of stress, this is an excellent resource for scientifically oriented readers who want to learn more about the stress response.

CHAPTER 2—Breathe Your Stress Away
- Donna Farhi, *The Breathing Book*, Henry Holt and Company, Inc., New York, 1996
This is a book on breathing for readers who want to explore this dimension more deeply. I have trained with the author and incorporate her teachings into my work.
- Rodney Yee, *Yoga: The Poetry of the Body*, Thomas Dunn Books, New York, 2002
I am including this book as a resource for this chapter because of its wonderful breathing exercises, but this book actually offers information that is applicable to all the chapters. The author is a phenomenal teacher with whom I've had the good fortune to study. I find inspiration in his teaching and his being.

CHAPTER 3—Soothe Those Frazzled Nerves

- Judith Lasater, Ph.D., P.T., *Relax & Renew: Restful Yoga for Stressful Times*, Rodmell Press, Berkeley, California, 1995

For readers who would enjoy more of the supported yoga postures offered in Chapter 3, this is an excellent book with which to expand your repertoire. It has been an invaluable resource for me over the years.

- Kathleen Cox, *The Power of Vastu Living*, Simon & Schuster, New York, 2002

This is a wonderful, clearly written book on incorporating the healing properties of the five elemental energies into our environment at home and at work.

CHAPTERS 4, 5, and 6—Positive Ways with Negative Feelings, Think Better and Feel Better, A New Look at Old Fears

- Jack Kornfield, *The Inner Art of Meditation*, Sounds True, Louisville, Colorado, 1993

This is a six-part audio study course on vipassana meditation with a world-renowned author and meditation teacher. I have benefited tremendously over the years from Dr. Kornfield's teachings. This is but one of his prolific works.

- Jack Kornfield, *Meditation for Beginners*, Sounds True, Louisville, Colorado, 2004

This book-and-CD combination is a much-abbreviated version of the set mentioned above, for the reader who wants only a taste rather than a full meal.

- Belleruth Naparstek, *Staying Well With Guided Imagery*, Warner Books, Inc., New York, 1994

For readers who enjoy using imagery, this book will deepen their understanding of the theory and practice of imagery work.

- Jeanne Achterberg, Ph.D., Barbara Dossey, R.N., M.S., FAAN, and Leslie Kolkmeier, R.N., Med., *Rituals of Healings*, Bantam Books, New York, 1994

This is a practical guide on using the power of imagination and rituals to help the body restore and maintain health. I have had the pleasure of attending Dr. Achterberg's workshops and I incorporate her teachings into my work.

- Harriet Lerner, Ph.D., *The Dance of Fear*, Harper Collins Publishers Inc., New York, 2004

This is a useful book for deepening your understanding of feelings. The author offers practical ways to overcome the feelings of anxiety, fear, and shame.

CHAPTER 7—The Road to Health and Wellness

- Dr. Vasant Lad, *Ayurveda: The Science of Self-Healing*, Lotus Press, Twin Lakes, Wisconsin, 1984

This practical and well-rounded guide clearly explains the principles and practical applications of Ayurveda, the oldest healing system in the world. This was the first book I read on the subject of Ayurveda, and it is still one of my favorite references. I have benefited from studying Ayurvedic principles as applied to the practice of yoga at the Ayurvedic Institute in Albuquerque, New Mexico, a school of Ayurveda founded by Dr. Lad.

- Dr. Vasant Lad, *Ayurveda: The Science of Life*, Sounds True, Louisville, Colorado, 1994

For readers who would rather listen than read, this six-part audio set helps them apply the Ayurveda system of total wellness to their lives.

- Maya Tiwari, *Ayurveda: A Life of Balance*, Healing Arts Press, Rochester, Vermont, 1995

This book is another of my favorite references. It includes recipes based on Ayurvedic principles, with notations of the energetic effects of the recipes.

- Mira Silva and Shyam Mehta, *Yoga the Iyengar Way*, Random House Inc., New York, 1990

This is a definitive book on Iyengar yoga, offering clear instructions with good illustrations. We recommend this book to beginning students at our yoga studio.

- Carol Blackman, M.A., and Elise Browning Miller, M.A., *Life is a Stretch: Easy Yoga Anytime, Anywhere*, Llewellyn Publications, St. Paul, Minnesota, 1999

This practical book offers simple and easy-to-do yoga poses to incorporate into busy lives. I have the pleasure of studying yoga with Elise Miller at every opportunity I can find.

CHAPTER 8—How to Sleep Better

- Deepak Chopra, M.D., *Restful Sleep*, Three Rivers Press, New York, 1991

This book is one of my primary sources for the material presented in this chapter. It would benefit readers who need more support in restoring normal sleep.

CHAPTER 9—Lose Weight and Keep it Off

- Deepak Chopra, M.D., *Perfect Weight*, Three Rivers Press, New York, 1994

This book is one of my primary sources for the material presented in this chapter. It would benefit readers who need more support to achieve and maintain an ideal weight.

CHAPTER 10—Final Ingredients for Low-Stress Living

- Rachel Schaeffer, *Yoga for Your Spiritual Muscles*, Theosophical Publishing House, Wheaton, Illinois, 1998

This interesting and unusual book weaves wisdom teachings and personal stories pertinent to contemporary life, with instructions for essential yoga postures.

- Jack Kornfield, *Your Buddha Nature*, Sounds True, Louisville, Colorado, 1997

This six-part audio set discusses the virtues of our essential nature and offers mindfulness techniques to help us open to them.

- Stephen Cope, *Yoga and the Quest for the True Self*, Bantam, New York, 1999

The author of this book, a Western-trained psychotherapist and a yoga teacher, shares his personal psychological and spiritual journey. I find this book a wonderful illustration of the process of self-inquiry and the nature of our essential selves.

- Swami Rama, Rudolph Ballentine, M.D., and Swami Ajaya, Ph.D., *Yoga and Psychotherapy*, Himalayan Institute, Honesdale, Pennsylvania, 1993

This book is an excellent reference for readers interested in a more in-depth analysis of how yoga and psychotherapy interface. The book is accessible to the layperson as well as the professional. ❧

INDEX

Eastern systems of medicine, 114–17. *See also* Ayurveda

eating. *See* diet

eating disorders, 152, 156

ego, 159, 174, 176

Emotional Freedom Techniques, 105

emotions, 24, 61–75, 86. *See also* anger; fear; feelings

    avoidance of, 61, 69, 86

    behavior and, 64–65

    children and, 62–63, 79

    conscious breathing and, 70–71

    cycle of, 80, 85, 95

    decision making and, 67–69

    as energy, 62–63, 70, 71, 73, 86

    environment and, 42

    flow of, 69, 73, 86

    identifying, 64–65, 73

    journaling and, 72–73

    letter writing and, 73–75

    managing, 61, 64, 66, 70, 72, 73, 75, 87

    negative, 65, 73, 82–83, 85, 95, 156

    positive, 66, 84

Emoto, Dr., 81

energy

    air, 141

    balance of, 116

    blocked, 61, 69, 70–71, 74, 97, 99–100

    daily routine and, 128–30

    earth, 128, 129, 140, 152, 153, 154

    fire, 117, 129, 140

    unblocking, 97, 105

    water, 128, 129, 153

energy exchange

    environment and, 40–42, 59

    people and, 40–41, 44, 45, 47

environment

    awareness and, 44

    detachment from, 108

    emotions and, 42

    energy exchange and, 40–42, 59

    sensory overload and, 39, 43–44, 59

    sleep patterns and, 141–42

ethical values, 167, 172–74

exercise, 126–28

    digestion and, 144

    sleep patterns and, 141, 144

    time between eating and, 160

    weight loss and, 154

    Western approach to, 126

exercises

    awareness, 23–24, 31–33, 42–43, 171, 174–75

    breath with movement, 49–55

    breathing, 31–36, 84

    leg stretches, 134, 136–37

    meditation, 91–93, 107–8

    reclining cobbler's pose, 57–58

    relaxation, 55–58, 145–47

    spinal, 131–34

    sun salutations, 160–65

    visualization, 93–95

Eye Movement Desensitization and Reprocessing, 105

fasting, 154–55

fatigue

    awareness of, 19, 158

    daily routines and, 120

    diet and, 123, 124

    relationships and, 79

    repressed feelings and, 69

Made in the USA